Have you suffered lately from cramps, nausea, vomiting or diarrhea? Call it "SUPERMARKET FLU"!

Jon A. McClure uncovers the corpses in the closets of America's largest supermarket chains: three clearly defined expendables called health, sanitation and safety. The blacklist of *The Jungle* is still strong within the meat-cutting vaults of our retail giants, and here is documented proof that they have plenty to hide: chuck sold as round steak; ground beef with 60 percent fat—the least nauseating and harmful of its adulterations; thawed and refrozen "fresh frozen" fish; scrubbed and repackaged slimy meats; bribed inspectors and much more.

Here is a tale of sodium sulphate, nitrites and nitrates, botulism, hepatitis, salmonella, shigella, dysentery, trichinosis and typhoid. The prescription? This book, which tells you how, where, what and when to buy for maximum safety and economy . . . and how to force strict legal controls over the moguls of retail marketing.

MEAT EATERS ARE THREATENED

JON A. McCLURE

 PYRAMID BOOKS • NEW YORK

CONDITIONS OF SALE

"Any sale, lease, transfer or circulation of this book by way of trade or in quantities of more than one copy, without the original cover bound thereon, will be construed by the Publisher as evidence that the parties to such transaction have illegal possession of the book, and will subject them to claim by the Publisher and prosecution under law."

MEAT EATERS ARE THREATENED

A PYRAMID BOOK

First printing, September 1973

ISBN 0-515-02984-X

Copyright © 1973 by Jon A. McClure
All Rights Reserved

Printed in the United States of America

Pyramid Books are published by Pyramid Communications, Inc. Its trademarks, consisting of the word "Pyramid" and the portrayal of a pyramid, are registered in the United States Patent Office.

PYRAMID COMMUNICATIONS, INC.
919 Third Avenue
New York, New York 10022, U.S.A.

To My Mother
  Who would have wanted
  this book written

> "We are carefully to preserve that life which the Author of Nature has given us, for it was no idle gift."
>
> HARVEY W. WILEY
> *First director of the
> Food and Drug Administration*

CONTENTS

Acknowledgments
Foreword

I	WHAT THEY DON'T KNOW WON'T HURT THEM	15
	It's Clean-Up Time	18
II	THE FRIENDLY MEAT INSPECTOR	20
	Our Little Price War	20
	The State Inspector Will Be in Tomorrow	21
	Ground Beef? Ground Chuck? Ground Round?	22
	The Deadly Delicatessen	23
	The Pay-off	26
	Fish, Anyone?	30
III	WHO SAYS THIS STORE ISN'T SAFE?	40
	This Store Is Wild	42
	Just How Wild?	43
	A Little Chicken Water Never Hurt Anyone	45
	Eeny, Meeny, Miny, Mo—Let's Make This Store Really Go	46
	What Do You Mean, This Store Isn't Safe?	46
	What Do You Mean, This Place Isn't Clean?	49
	Raw Pork Won't Hurt You, Much!	57
	You Can't Take Pictures in a Meat Market	60
IV	THE APPRENTICESHIP	65
	You Just Caught the "Bug"—That's All, Honey	67
	This Stuff Is "Dynamite"	73
	We're Number Three, But We Try Harder	74
	The Independent Food Store	77
V	THE HOG	80
	Hams Ain't What They Used To Be	85
VI	THE REAL JUNGLE	89
	They May Be Number Three—But Watch Out!	90
	The Little Meat Processor	91
	What Did You Say Your Animal Died Of?	94
	We've Come a Long Way Over the Years— Haven't We?	96

VII	WHOLESALE VERSUS RETAIL	101
	What's Happening in Retail	108
	Wholesale Sanitation Checks	109
	I Wonder What Goes on Back There	110
	The Wholesale Business Has Come a Long Way	111
VIII	THE GROSS PROFIT PICTURE	113
	The Companies Keep the Public in the Dark	114
	You Can't Merchandise a Can of Beans?	114
	Gross: Makes a Busy Man Happy	116
	Oh! That Inventory Control	119
	Pork Sausages: a High-Profit Item	120
	Temperature Control Is Important	120
IX	WEIGHTS AND MEASURES—HA!	122
	Weights and Measures Do Affect Gross Profit	124
	The Hand Is Quicker than the Eye	126
	What Happened to Inspection?	127
	Watch Them When They Cut Your Side Order	128
	Maybe Things Will Get Better—Someday?	129
X	LET'S HOPE WE DON'T BECOME WHAT WE EAT	129
XI	COMMENTS AND RECOMMENDATIONS	136
	What Can the State Do?	136
	What Can the Consumer Do Now?	138
	What the Consumer Ought to Know	138
	Meat Deli Check List	142
	Frozen Food Check List	144
	When to Buy	144
	Where to Buy	145
	What Should the Retail Meat Establishment Do?	147
	What Could Comprise a Comprehensive Health and Sanitation Program?	147
	Advice to the Consumer	149
	Let's Stop Polluting Our Bodies	151
	FOLLOW-UP READING	153
	NOTES	155

ACKNOWLEDGMENTS

My thanks to the many meat cutters who signed statements disclosing public abuse by retail supermarkets. Many of the tradesmen have large families, and they had mixed emotions about signing, for fear of losing their jobs and being blackballed from the trade through corporate power. Special thanks to those men with families who did sign, and to the men and women who made further sworn testimony before my lawyer.

I would like to thank my lawyer, Joseph Steinberg, for his patience, consideration and guidance in the writing of this manuscript.

My gratitude to Dr. Frank Chrienza, dean of Arts and Sciences at the University of Hartford, for encouraging me in the beginning; to my colleagues and my former boss, Dr. Daniel Viamonte, chairman of the Speech and Drama Department at the University of Hartford, for their encouragement; to Dr. Wade C. Curry, acting dean of Arts and Sciences at Trenton State College, for his comments.

And finally I would like to thank Dr. Norman A. Heap, chairman of the Speech and Theater Department at Trenton State College, for his interest and encouragement.

Foreword

On July 29, 1971, I had a phone conversation with a nineteen-year-old girl who was working in a supermarket meat delicatessen. I asked her if she would tell an attorney some of the conditions that existed in the meat market where she worked. Her mother, who was on the extension, was very quick to reply, "I know the conditions were terrible, but we don't want her to get involved." The young girl said she had just finished a college course that convinced her that big companies have a way of making it difficult to get a job. She didn't want to jeopardize her future. I said she would be protected by the union and the courts. She was sorry, but she was frightened.

A similar conversation was repeated with a young boy who complained for four months about the terrible adulterations in meats, salads, and puddings in the markets in Wethersfield, Connecticut. He wrote a personal letter describing the poor sanitary conditions in the meat deli. He later signed a letter describing further the unhealthy conditions, but when asked to talk to a lawyer, he replied, "I talked it over with my parents, and I don't think so." His mother's reply was "Let someone else do it; we don't want him to get involved."

This book started in 1961, while I was working as an apprentice meat cutter in Missouri and Kansas. The research work continued over a period of ten years, during which I worked in 60 supermarkets of 8 different companies.

It's difficult to believe that there is no mention of health and sanitation procedures in the customer policy statement, which hangs in the front of almost every store from coast to coast. This is also true of other chains and independents throughout the country. But certain questions must arise: What is going on behind the partition in the meat departments where you buy your meat? Doesn't the public have the right to know about the adulterations in meat which affect their health and their pocketbooks?

Many people say, "Oh, that couldn't happen in little old Cloverville, or Simsbury." But it is happening. I have seen meat mishandled in over 60 stores in Missouri, Kansas, and most recently, in Connecticut.

On July 6, 1971, I was fired from a market which is operated by a large national chain. I had photographed the meat department and its lack of sanitation as documentation for this book. The official dismissal was on the grounds that it was against company policy to take pictures without permission in any of its meat departments.

The retail meat departments' feelings toward their customers are not truly reflected in those nice little signs worn by the meat cutters—"WE CARE." Perhaps the best example of the way some companies feel about their customers could be expressed in this meaty story:

> It seems there was a meat department advertising "Government-inspected 50% pure rabbitburger." When the customer asked how the store could sell rabbitburger so cheap, the meat manager said, "I have to put in some horse meat too. But I mix them fifty-fifty—one horse, one rabbit."

At first people rationalize when they get a rotten piece of meat. They think the guy down the street will give them a better deal for their money, but they soon find out that the guy down the street is just like the guy up the street. In fact, since he is a smaller operator, he is forced to pay more for the same merchandise, because he orders in lesser quantities. To survive, the smaller stores have to cheat just a little more than the big ones do.

Many small stores do well until a new, larger supermarket opens next door. Then the large store wages a price war against the smaller store, and the smaller store dies. You can see this small store in your neighborhood. It's been converted into a shoe store, a theater, a bowling alley, or an automotive parts store. This is called "survival of the fittest."

But for some reason even the largest and strongest must continue to fight each other. This is another facet of the system. One chain fights another chain, and both are so large that neither is hurt. But there are victims. The unions negotiate for raises. To maintain their profit margin, the companies raise the prices or cut the man-hours. Raising the prices may lose customers to the competition. So they cut man-hours.

But the stores must still process the same amount of meat. There are, however, some items that stores consider expendable—health, sanitation, and safety. Prices are kept down by running machines continuously, rather than stopping occasionally to clean them. Employees are constantly prodded and coerced by management to cut more and more, faster and faster. Knives fly and fingers are slashed. Sanitation codes are ignored. The result is cheaper, adulterated meat, a filthy workroom, and scared workers.

Few people outside the meat business know this, and it's doubtful that a worker in the trade will stand up to management, for it is his word against theirs. Even if he could prove his claim, he would be blackballed from his job as a journeyman meat cutter. Companies have a way of taking care of people who cause trouble. So the meat cutter feels he must do what management tells him. His family comes first. This is the way man is—this is survival. And there is little the consumer can do. He must buy meat or become a vegetarian.

Chapter I

WHAT THEY DON'T KNOW WON'T HURT THEM

"Oh, my God, Sherye's cut herself! Jon, run up front to get some Band-Aids. Quick! Try to get some gauze and tape."

I ran over to the meat scale and saw that Sherye had cut her finger clear to the bone. There was no way that we could stop the blood. I raced to the front of the store and grabbed two packages of gauze, but before I could go back to the meat department, I had to get an O.K. from the store manager. I then went back to the meat department and we ripped the gauze open, wrapped Sherye's finger and rushed her off to the hospital. We later found out that her husband would not let her come back there to work again. The cut was so severe that a skin graft was necessary.

Paul, a co-worker, said to me, "Tomorrow it's going to be one of us, because this place is just too damn small."

This incident occurred in April 1971, in a large national chain supermarket in Wethersfield, Connecticut. There are 12 meat department personnel in this supermarket. We work in a small area, no more than 8 feet wide. It's long, approximately 60 feet. But it's the narrow width that can kill you.

As you come out of the cooler with a slab of meat and look down the cutting room, you see a line of white smocks with arms protruding from them, working at a feverish pace. No time to look up, no time for conversation. Each time you go back to the cooler to get another piece of meat, you must needle your way

16 / Meat Eaters are Threatened

around twelve 6-foot-long stainless steel tree hooks with rounds, chucks, and loins hanging at an angle and therefore protruding. As you work your way through this mass of meat and steel, you are likely to rip your smock on the bones or the needle-sharp points of the hooks. If you are lucky, you will make it into the rear cooler without a stainless steel hook in your back.

Once you get to the meat cooler, you then go through the meticulous process of selecting the appropriate piece of meat, which must be picked up and lugged back to your cutting block through the jungle of hooks and bones.

Each move must be taken very carefully. "Watch Out!" "I am behind you!" "Watch Out!" As you walk by the meat cutters, you pray that one of the men in white doesn't turn around with his knife in his hand.

All the while, the sounds of the district man are heard, "Paul, give me four center-cut pork chops, one-half inch thick. Terry, what are you doing? I told you to chime that bone, not cut clear into it. Chime it! Tony, I told you to cut half loins. Now, this half loin is going to be a little too big for the customer's broiler pan, so let's cut chops out of it. O.K.?"

"But isn't that cheating the customer?"

"No, it really isn't cheating the customer. This loin is too big for the customer's broiler pan anyway."

"O.K., whatever you say; you're the boss." Jobs are always hard to get.

Looking down toward the end of the cutting room, you see six girls trying to get the meat wrapped, reaching up and lifting the pans off the conveyor line. They're trying to work as fast as their arms will permit. The meat manager comes charging in and yells at the girls, "Who's the idiot that fouled up all these prices? Come over here! From now on each one of you girls will have a code number on the machine and the number will correspond with you. This way, we catch mistakes and know who did it. No more guessing." He stomps out of the room, leaving the girls frightened and frustrated, causing them to be hesitant about weighing from that point on. They act like a bunch of pups that were whipped with a newspaper. They had done something wrong, and now they are reluctant to take over the position of running the automatic weighing machine, for each time they make a mistake, they will be severely criticized for it. A small mistake, particularly in the vital pricing area, seems to be a capital offense.

At the end of the cooler is a very large stainless steel sink that stretches some 5 feet across. In the bottom of the sink are 12 or 14 smoked picnic hams, just lying there, though the sink is full of detergent. There are also three pairs of blood-soaked gloves, six filthy aluminum pans, four meat scrapers and—lying back in the corner underneath the pans, soaking up water like a sponge—a very large halibut fish. I notice that I am standing on something, and underneath my work shoes I find two herring fish. As I pick up the fish, I discover an entire box of herring lying in about 2 inches of stagnant water next to the drain. I turn around and ask the men what to do with the fish. They say, "Don't worry about them; just throw them back into the box. What you don't know won't hurt you."

That seemed to be a cliché around there: "What you don't know won't hurt you." Another very popular cliché when you drop a piece of meat in the sawdust is, "Charge extra for this one; it's breaded."

You wonder how any employee can stand buying meat from any meat case after seeing things like this almost daily.

After the day crew goes home (usually between five and six in the evening), the night crew takes over—four people. Their job is to make sure that they keep the cases filled and that they set up for the day people. The night crew work from 5 p.m. to closing time. A day never goes by without the night crew's being criticized for not doing enough. But, again, when the supervisor can no longer find things wrong with their work, he will be out of a job. Yet it is a wrong and outdated notion that an attitude of fear must be passed down from the top echelon through the ranks in order to maintain steady productivity.

It's Clean-Up Time

Let's follow a night crew. Walk carefully. There is usually so much grease, fat, and suet ground into the cement floor that it feels like an ice-skating rink. As you teeter-totter your way from one cutting block to the next, throwing soap on the blocks to clean them, scraping the blood and fat onto the floor, you wonder just how long this place will stay open before the health department closes it. You wonder how they have managed to stay open this long. The blocks have not been lifted from their steel frames and cleaned properly for the last two months. The crew started to lift the blocks up last night to clean them, but they ran out of time. Although the smell was so putrid it could make you vomit, they put the tops back on and left them for another night.

Their work load, once again on that night, had not given them enough time to clean the market properly. The power saws were still dirty. They merely scraped the bone dust out of the bottom catchall pan and wiped off the top. They never got to the pools of blood and fat inside the saws.

The night crew must now start scraping up a black substance from the floors. It's unique to the meat-cutting industry. Granular in nature, it emits a cloud of grey dust when it is first dropped on the floor. When water and blood are added, it turns into a very dark, crusty type of mud. This substance is known as "kitty litter." Although the state says that "sawdust is unsanitary," the market still uses it and resorts to the kitty litter only when the supply of sawdust runs out. The kitty litter is dumped into an empty chicken box and carried out to the trash receptacle. The crew dumped 12 small bone barrels into larger 55-gallon barrels and pushed them through the cutting room and meat cooler, where they will be picked up by the rendering company. Because the meat cooler is so small, we cannot help scraping thousands of pounds of meat with the bone barrels as we push them through the length of the cooler. As we look back at the meat, we see rust and dirt covering the surfaces.

One night, because of the emphasis on production and the lack of concern about safety or cleanliness, the knife guards had not been put up on the meat blocks. Instead, the knives were placed about 4 feet above the tops of the blocks where the food trays were stored. While straightening out the food trays, a 5-inch boning knife fell directly between my arms and stabbed into the top of the block right next to my belt buckle. There is no reason why this same incident will not happen again tomorrow, for the knife racks will still be lying on top of the trays. This reflects management's lack of concern for the employees' health and safety. Very few safety measures are taken, but if the placement of knife racks could increase production, I am certain that they would be installed immediately.

It seems that everything is done for profit and production, and nothing for the employee and the public.

CHAPTER II

THE FRIENDLY MEAT INSPECTOR

The Wethersfield supermarket was doing a land-office business. But once the grand opening was over, the company started cutting help. They cut 50 man-hours one week and decided to cut another 40 man-hours the following week. This went on for about two months. It was all we could do just to keep the meat case covered with a few packages of meat.

What little clean-up had been done before now disappeared completely. All we had time for was to take out the trash, scrape off the top of the saw, and rake the sawdust. The saws, the blocks, and the floor were all so contaminated with decomposed meat that the smell in the cutting room made us sick.

Our Little Price War

A competing supermarket opened next door, and the action was on. A large national supermarket chain company, which owns the store, waged a price war against the other. Call them "A" and "B". Everytime "B" lowered its prices, "A" would go a penny below. The customers came from all over for the "bargains." But what seemed to be bargains were not really bargains at all. The steaks were cheaper than those in most places in town, but the fat and the bone content were excessive. The ground beef was a joke. If "B" reduced their "G.B." (ground beef) from, for example, 68 cents a pound to 58 cents a pound, we would cut our price to 57 cents, one penny under theirs. Their supervisors visited our store, and our supervisors visited theirs. In conversation the supervisors would say, "Our ground beef is leaner than theirs, and did you get a look at the fat on those steaks?" A similar conversation must have taken place in the "B" market. The employees from each store would exchange visits. As the "G.B." war continued, you wouldn't have needed meat cutters' credentials to see what was happening. The prices continued to fall: if they cut to, say, 55 cents a pound, we cut to 48 cents a pound. This had to be the rock-bottom price, as we were selling below cost. (These prices are not accurate. This is only an example to show the reader the kind of thing that goes on between competitors.) In respect to quality we had reached rock bottom too. The fat content was about 60 percent, about twice the maximum allowable by federal and state standards.

"The State Inspector Will Be in Tomorrow"

The meat inspector had not checked the meat market for months. One day the meat manager came to me and said, "Listen, Jon, I want this entire place cleaned up. I want the floor swept and the mill torn down and cleaned. Wash the conveyor line. I want this place immaculate. The state inspector will be in tomorrow." When I asked how he knew, he replied with a smile, "I just have a feeling." The meat market was cleaned by five of the personnel.

We worked long into the night on an emergency clean-up operation. The next day, in the early afternoon, the day before Easter, a state inspector walked through the door.

He checked packages for the proper weight and tested one package of ground beef, which was found to contain 29 percent fat, one percent below the state maximum for fat content. The inspector did not check the saws, the ground beef mill, the blocks, the bone barrels, or anything else, as far as we could tell. Two employees witnessed the entire inspection.[1]

Meat inspections, whether federal or state, are legally required to be on an unwarned basis. If they are not, there is no point in having inspections. When the markets are warned, there is no need to spend money and man-hours on normal clean-up schedules. This practice probably occurs all over the United States. It has occurred in about 10 of the 60 stores I have worked in over the past ten years. The head meat cutter receives a phone call telling him the store will be inspected. He has time to get rid of adulterated meat and to set his house in order.

The Task Force on Environmental Health and Related Problems has pointed out some alarming facts to the Secretary of Health, Education and Welfare. It has seemed that many products available on the market, both household and food items, are processed or manufactured in ways that render them hazardous to humans under normal use, and at present there aren't adequate means of protecting the consumer.[2] Inspectors who take payoffs are merely adding to the public dilemma.

The frightening thought is that even with a day's advance notice and an emergency clean-up, the market wouldn't have passed a *careful* inspection. And what adulterations the state would have found if the inspection had been unwarned!

Ground Beef? Ground Chuck? Ground Round?

The government standard of 30 percent fat content in ground beef is much too generous. While fat is a natural constituent of all meat and does contribute to flavor and juiciness, it does not abound in nutrients. In fact, its major contribution is calories. Most of the fat turns to grease when ground beef is cooked. With excessive fat present, the customer is cheated in price and nutrition. The fat is taking up the space that could be occupied by protein.

Aside from fat content, *Consumer Reports* in August 1971 hinted that samples of ground beef, ground chuck, and ground round on some occasions are about the same thing, and yet the customer is paying more for the chuck and the round. In my experience ground chuck and ground round very often turned out to be the same thing in most stores. The only difference is that sometimes ground round may be leaner. Ground round is rarely ground round as the name implies, nor is ground chuck really ground chuck. They are a combination of lean trimmings, shank, and neck meat. If stores have some roast or steaks which seem too dark to sell, they will bone them out for chuck or round. If the meat has an excessive amount of fat, the stores hide this fat with blood. They use the neck, the last part of the animal to hold blood, because it is bled with the neck down. The neck is put in the grind, saturating the fat with red blood. It looks fine and it's done every day.

The Deadly Delicatessen

The "Meat Deli" in that Wethersfield supermarket surpassed the meat department in poor health and poor sanitation.

The following is from a letter signed by four employees who worked in that meat deli.

> The Deli Department sells cold cuts, desserts, salads and cheeses. The cases that contain the meats and other items mentioned are not being cleaned properly and consequently there is bacteria growth, which is evident from the tremendous odors coming from the cases. All of these items are contained in the same case and there are

no covers on the desserts or salads; thus there is nothing to stop the free movement of bacteria from meats to desserts. Perhaps the greatest hazard to the customers' health is the improper cleaning of utensils and slicing machines. Slicing machines are not being cleaned every night and in many cases they go for three or four days before being cleaned. This is because management expects you to finish your job assignments. They could fire you if you don't do the job. The employee feels management is remiss, for they have not stressed clean-up; so this is the one thing you don't do; this is the only thing you can get away with.

Management constantly tells you the customer comes first; this can only be a lie after seeing how remiss they are in health and sanitation practices. The white smock and the stainless steel tops are a false front, a façade which makes the customer believe he is being treated fairly. The truth is they are being deceived in the worst way. Nothing is more important in the handling and processing of meats and prepared foods than sanitation and health and yet this is management's least concern for the customer.

All of the above statements are true and we feel they must stop for the health and protection of the consuming public. We know they are true for we have worked in the forementioned meat deli.[3]

Many states require a health card for anyone working in the preparation or handling of food items. To get a food card, the worker must pass a complete physical examination. However, none of the personnel who signed this letter had ever been given a physical examination to see if they were carrying any communicable diseases.

The Friendly Meat Inspector / 25

Suppose one of the four employees had hepatitis. It's common enough. A customer orders a pound of potato salad. While dipping up the salad, the employee coughs, and some of the germs get in the salad. Let's say the customer is going for a picnic at a state park that is a two-hour drive away. In transit the germs start to grow by the millions. Let's assume the men start playing ball after arrival at the park, so it will still be another hour or two before lunch. Finally, after four hours on a pleasant, 90-degree afternoon, the salad is eaten. Someone may very well contract hepatitis from eating the potato salad. Tuberculosis, typhoid fever, and staphylococcal food poisoning can be contracted in the same way.

The spores have no odor. They were given a chance to multiply over a period of about four hours in very favorable conditions. It's not certain how many millions or billions of spores developed. The Department of Health, Education and Welfare has reported that in twenty-four hours under favorable conditions a single spore could produce 281,000,000,000,000 other spores with every one capable of spreading the disease. The report states:

> People have died because they ate and drank heartily, trusting in those who prepared and served the food. And people will continue to sicken and die because they eat out, unless you protect them. You cannot always tell by tasting whether food is safe or not.[4]

There are thousands of employees presently working in meat departments and meat delis throughout the United States who have not been given a physical specifically to see if they are disease spreaders. I have not been asked to take a physical since 1961.

Many people feel that compulsory health examinations for food handlers are not enough. Chest x-rays, mouth smears, and blood serologies cannot be the complete answer in cutting down on the spread of disease through food handlers. What is needed is a program which educates all food handlers to the dangers of "staph" (staphylococcal food poisoning), typhoid, dysentery, salmonella, and other types of food-borne disease. Obviously an annual physical cannot protect the public from a disease acquired in the middle of the year. Yet if a physical examination finds only a few cases of syphilis, tuberculosis, hepatitis, or other serious diseases, annual examinations would seem justified. But is it really so? What is needed is a joint program of education to make the employees aware of the need for proper care of food, and a complete physical examination.

In the past ten years I have not seen or heard one film, lecture, or discussion in the sanitary care or handling of meat. The major food chains and independent stores in this country seem to have no interest in safeguarding the public health. And state and local authorities have their hands tied.

The Payoff

The U. S. Department of Agriculture is responsible for inspection in the interstate packing houses; the intrastate packing houses are mostly inspected by the state authorities. Local health departments and state health departments are responsible for inspecting supermarkets. The local health departments don't seem to check supermarkets with much scrutiny. The state health departments try, but occasionally incidents like the one described in the following excerpt from a letter frustrate the legitimate intent of the law.

> Today the state inspector, —— ——, came into the ——— market, where he was given two

large barrel bags. One bag was full of meat that was not priced; this bag was given to him by the meat manager. The other bag was given to the inspector by the produce manager; it was full of unmarked produce.

The inspector talked to the store manager for approximately twenty minutes before leaving. The merchandise was not paid for and there was no inspection of the store.

Furthermore, he did not even go into the meat cooler or cutting room. This practice is illegal and must stop for the protection and interest of the customers."[5]

This incident was witnessed by three employees. The meat inspector's name was left blank in the letter, because one inspector's taking a bribe should not detract from the good that the Connecticut Consumer Protection Division has done over the years. I have seen constant payoffs in 10 of the 60 stores I worked in. Many of the inspectors were journeyman meat cutters before they took the inspector jobs, and for several years they must take a cut in pay, which may be very difficult for a family man with three or four children.

A study of state and local food and drug programs in 1965 showed that many of the state food and drug personnel had less than a high school education, that 41 percent of the state milk and dairy supervisors, 71 percent of food inspection supervisory personnel, and 84 percent of the weights and measures supervisory personnel had no college degree.[6] With the present pay scale for inspectors in Connecticut, it would be difficult to attract qualified college graduates. Meat inspectors are starting at Grade One with $8,222, advancing to a top inspector's salary of $10,322 a year.

This low pay scale could only encourage corruption. This is demonstrated by a case in New York where 21 milk firms, including a large number of major distributors in the metropolitan area, were indicted in 1968 for paying off sanitarians. A couple of the men had been working on the job for forty and twenty-five years, respectively. In the Grand Jury investigation, District Attorney Hogan's office said, "payments had been made to inspectors to overlook Health Department standards."[7]

It's difficult to determine where to place the blame—on the inspector taking a bribe or on the company giving it. But each time a bribe takes place, the victim is the consumer.

The Model State Meat and Poultry Products Inspection Act for the state of Connecticut makes it quite clear who is legally guilty in a case of bribery:

> Any person who gives, pays or offers, directly or indirectly, to any officer or employee of this state authorized to perform any of the duties prescribed by this act or by the regulations of the commissioner, any money or other thing of value, with intent to influence such officer or employee in the discharge of any such duty, shall be fined not more than five thousand dollars or be imprisoned not more than three years, or both; and any officer or employee of this state authorized to perform any of the duties prescribed by this act who accepts any money, gift or other thing of value from any person, given with intent to influence his official action, or who receives or accepts from any person engaged in intrastate commerce any gift, money or other thing of value given with any purpose or intent whatsoever, shall upon conviction thereof, be summarily discharged from office and shall be fined not more than five thousand dollars or be imprisoned not more than three years, or both.[8]

The last time the meat inspector came in, management was so confident that they didn't even bother to have the meat market cleaned. There was trash, meat, and sawdust all over the floor, covering a distance of about 60 square feet. A few chickens had fallen on the floor, and no one had had time to pick them up. Meat trays and food containers were spread over the floor as if they were also trash.

The market should have been condemned, and surely any meat inspector who wasn't taking a bribe would have closed it. Unfortunately for the public, this meat inspector had formerly been employed by the chain. That is where his friends work, and therefore each time he inspects their stores, he overlooks a great many things. He was obviously disgusted with the condition of the meat department, and he did say, "This place looks like a — house." But then he just turned around and walked out.

He doesn't take bribes from all companies, nor does he call up the four other large food chains in the area, to warn them of a meat inspection. However, this partisan relationship will eventually destroy him. It is just a matter of time before the other companies get the word. When this happens, the customers throughout his inspection area will have no one to protect them. This man may have lost all of his self-respect by now, so a bribe from another company should be easy.

Similar incidents and conditions exist throughout the country, and it is time that the public demand strict supervision from the companies, the cities, the states, and the federal government. The short periods of time the inspectors spend in retail supermarkets can't allow them an opportunity to see the constant flagrant abuses which take place. Many abuses are deliberate, carefully thought out, and very difficult to detect.

Fish, Anyone?

One of the most common and deliberate abuses, and one which may cause serious sickness, occurs every night in the Wethersfield market.

Whoever works the late shift must pull all the thawed frozen fish out of the fresh meat case and put them in the freezer case. The next day the same fish—now solidly refrozen—are taken out of the frozen food case and put back in the fresh meat case. This goes on for months, so the same fish may be thawed out and refrozen hundreds of times. With this continuous thawing and refreezing, many strange things take place inside the tissues of that dead fish.

Store abuse in handling fish is not the only problem for fish eaters. There is mishandling before the fish even reach the store, and another problem: pollution. In testimony before the Consumer Subcommittee of the Senate Committee on Commerce, Dr. Philip R. Lee, Assistant Secretary of Health and Scientific Affairs (HEW), said, "Infectious hepatitis has been linked to shellfish in four different incidents since 1964. A total of 309 cases of hepatitis have been traced to shellfish from four eastern coastal areas."[9] Those are reported cases—no one knows the number of unreported illnesses associated with eating fish. Some fresh clams caught off the New Jersey Coast as recently as 1971 were proven to be contaminated by water pollution. "Clearly, unless consumer protection methods are strengthened, further cases of disease or death may be anticipated."[10]

In 1966 about 400 cases of salmonella food poisoning, attributed to smoked fish, were reported in one weekend. The same year 250 cases of food poisoning, 12 from imported shrimp, were recorded in a single city. "Several cases of botulism have been attributed to poisoned fish products over the years."[11]

The Friendly Meat Inspector / 31

Quality standards for fish and fishery products do not exist. In testimony before the Consumer Subcommittee of the Senate Committee on Commerce, Harold E. Crowther, Director of the Bureau of Commercial Fisheries, said in July 1967:

Fish and fishery products must be given proper care and handling, for they are perishable items. There has been improvement over the years by a state inspection, the Public Health Services Shellfish Inspection, the Departments' Voluntary Inspection Program and actions of the Food and Drug Administration, but much more needs to be done if fish products are to receive the trust comparable to competitive meats and poultry items. While meat and poultry consumption is increasing, fish and fishery products consumption has remained static over the past two decades. Part of the problem is lack of confidence in the quality of fish products.[12]

There is much mishandling before the fish even gets to the supermarket. It may take a trawler weeks to completely fill its hold while the fish is eviscerated, washed, and packed down with ice. The fish near the bottom suffer much abuse from the weight of other fish, water, and ice. It is a miracle if the fish can make it back to the coast area and still be referred to as fresh fish.

Deterioration in fish is rapid, and while the fish is in transit from ship to packing plant, deterioration is taking place. Even after being processed and packed, it may end up defrosting, again in transit, while sitting on a loading dock ready for truck shipment. Later it is refrozen slowly in the refrigerated truck—favorable conditions for bacteria build-up. The truck drops the fish off at a distributor warehouse, where it may thaw again, only to be refrozen in the warehouse freezer. Finally, another truck picks up the same fish and takes it to a supermarket, where it usually sits from thirty minutes to four hours before it is properly stored. In Missouri and Kansas I have seen frozen fish left overnight in unrefrigerated night storage areas on scores of occasions. This is a very common occurrence and it is quite simple just to refreeze the fish. No one will know.

The fish orders in some Connecticut supermarkets owned by this chain are unloaded into grocery carts or four-wheeled pushcarts, where they usually sit, unrefrigerated, next to the delivery door for several hours before they are priced and put in the freezer case to be once again refrozen. The October, 1967 issue of *Consumer Reports* had an article on samples of frozen foods saying, "Many of the dinners we examined and tasted this time appear to have been shipped, handled or stored in ways that permitted their temperatures to rise well above those required to maintain quality and guarantee wholesomeness."[13]

The poor handling that frozen fish products receive causes the fish to lose their moisture. They become tough and dry and usually change color. Because much of the frozen fish is breaded, the poor quality is hard to detect. The fish may even be rancid and unfit for human consumption. *Consumer Reports* in September, 1970 indicated that there are some very serious problems because of improper handling of frozen foods before they reach the consumer. In 1970 *Consumer Reports* stated "Now, nine years later, CU must report with regret that progress in the regulation of the manufacture and marketing of this product has been virtually nil since 1961."[14] Two years later, the June 1972 issue of *Consumer Reports* stated, "In all our tests of frozen fish and shellfish, we have found that time and poor temperature control took a heavy toll on quality. In one instance, CU shoppers found Birds Eye frozen fish sticks on sale a year after General Foods had stopped making them."[15]

Another common occurrence that affects the consumer is refrigeration breakdown in the supermarkets. I personally have restocked about fifty frozen food cases due to maintenance difficulties. Ice builds up around the freezer fans and eventually they stop, causing a freezer breakdown. This is an everyday occurrence throughout the United States, and it will continue unless new freezer concepts are developed.

But the problem of constant mishandling would remain. There is also danger from human contamination; in many cases when fish thaws, the moisture breaks through the package, and someone must rewrap it.

The Association of Food and Drug Officials of the United States adopted a code in 1961 requiring constant temperature control at zero degrees Fahrenheit or lower for frozen products at each stage of handling.[16] The reason for this requirement is that frozen food products stored at over zero degrees deteriorate relatively rapidly even if they are not once thawed and refrozen. This code has not been properly observed since its adoption in 1960.

The illnesses associated with fish products were primarily hepatitis, salmonella, and shigella. Some of the fears because of inadequate inspection of fish products were brought out in testimony by James L. Goddard, Commissioner of Food and Drugs during the hearings in 1968 for implementation of the Wholesome Fish and Fishery Products Act. The proceedings of this consumer Subcommittee and many other similar hearings may be more important than Watergate to many Americans in the future because they affect the health of all of us. During the hearings Dr. Goddard indicated that hepatitis was the most common disease contracted from the ingestion of shell fish from contaminated waters.[17] Hepatitis, which means inflammation of the liver, is a very serious disease. Cases of this disease have risen sharply in America since World War II.[18]

As the table here shows, the cases of a number of food-borne diseases have been increasing in the past ten years. The state of Connecticut was chosen because health conditions there are typical of those in the country.

There is another problem which doesn't affect the safety or wholesomeness of fish products but does affect the taste. Because of mishandling, the fish become stale and develop undesirable flavors. When the fish is frozen and thawed and refrozen again, the natural oils deteriorate, giving the fish rancid flavor.

We pollute the waters with mercury, pesticides, oil, and even low-level radioactive waste, and eventually the effects of this pollution work their way through the food chain to man. But perhaps no risk to our food supply is as deliberate as the poor care which fresh and frozen fish products receive when they reach modern supermarkets. Supermarkets hold the consumers' health in their hands. They are the last major threat before product purchases. Proper supermarket screening and proper supermarket handling could do much to avoid unnecessary tragedies.

The retail meat departments in the United States, in their handling of clams, shrimp, lobsters, oysters, crabs, and all other shellfish, are contributing to a regression of public health standards. These items may harbor infectious organisms that are difficult to detect—but deadly to the consumer.

Other types of fish products prepared in meat delicatessens may be even more harmful. Again, the company's real concern is gross profit, not consumer protection. Pickled fish, fresh fish, and meat and fish salads are kept in the same deli case with cole slaw, potato salad, macaroni salad, and all types of dessert items, including rice pudding and tapioca pudding. Few of these

REPORTED CASES OF FOOD-BORNE DISEASES IN CONNECTICUT, 1961-1970

Disease	1961	1962	1963	1964	1965	1966	1967	1968	1969	1970
Shigella, dysentery (bacillary)	32	76	142	90	59	44	83	121	72	83
Food poisoning	25	89	65	20	107	173	26	137	390	457
Hepatitis, including serum hepatitis	483	398	616	667	315	349	638	629	756	1056
Salmonella infections	99	96	184	433	252	235	226	211	269	327
Trichinosis	33	20	5	9	14	11	1	2	1	5
Typhoid fever	3	0	7	3	2	4	3	3	5	4

items are covered. The odors and the bacteria move freely from one container to another. Very seldom are any of these items thrown away. New quantities are added to them. A customer may be buying pudding that is several months old. It may not be contaminated, but paying good money for a stale product that is represented as being fresh is an insult. Besides, the product necessarily picks up the odors from the strong spices, onions, vinegar, and pickling solutions found in the meats and salads.

At the end of the week all the deli items in the supermarket where I worked were taken out of the deli case and put in a large, enclosed back-up cooler, which had not been cleaned for six months. This was the same cooler where chickens were stored after being cut and wrapped. Unfortunately, chickens have a tendency to leak through the bottom of the package, so drippings fall into the puddings, salads, and fish products. This provides a perfect setting for food poisoning to develop. This process was observed for six months without change. There is no way of telling whether people contracted food poisoning from this unhealthy practice. Employees have complained about these and many other conditions in the supermarket, but the management has little concern for substantially improving the health and sanitary conditions at the present time.

It is hoped that new laws will be enacted to rectify these and other unscrupulous conditions existing in the retail food industry.

One such law that many consumer-rights advocates feel would help is the Wholesome Fish and Fishery Products Bill. This bill is intended to regulate interstate commerce by amending the Federal Food, Drug and Cosmetic Act to provide inspection of facilities used in the harvesting and processing of fish and fishery products for commercial purposes. The bill is also intended to regulate inspection of fish and fishery products and to work in cooperation with the states in the intrastate commerce and inspection programs.

Betty Furness, Special Assistant to the President for Consumer Affairs, in a letter included in the July 1968 hearings before the Consumer Subcommittee of the Senate Committee on Commerce, felt the bill had merits.

She indicated in the letter that food poisoning attributed to fish is partly the fault of inadequate inspection and surveillance. Insufficient laboratory facilities, insufficient personnel for inspections, and lack of comprehensive regulatory authority cause this situation.

Another proponent of the Wholesome Fish bill is Dr. Philip R. Lee, who is, as mentioned earlier, Assistant Secretary for Health Education and Scientific Affairs of HEW. Dr. Lee stated:

> Over the last few years, there has been growing public concern for greater protection of the American consumer from unsanitary, adulterated or misbranded foods—especially meats, poultry and fish.
>
> The conditions we have found include:
>
> Vessels improperly equipped and maintained to handle and preserve the fish catch in a sanitary manner. For example, inadequate facilities to keep the fish iced and use of polluted water to wash boats and fish.
>
> Improper practices in unloading the fish. For example, allowing fish to sit on docks in open boxes in the sunlight for long periods of time, thus accelerating decomposition and allowing contamination by birds and other animals. Also the use of pitchforks in unloading the fish.
>
> Grossly insanitary [sic] conditions and improper controls in processing plants. For example, failure to keep the establishments clean and clear

of debris or refuse, as well as external influences such as fly and roach infestations which attack the fish during its processing. Also failure to control properly sterilization and can-closing operations.

Improper sanitation measures employed by employees in fish processing plants. For example, employees' failure to wash their hands after handling dirty objects such as garbage cans and employees returning fish that have dropped on the floor to the processing line.[19]

Dr. Lee feels that improper handling after processing may contribute to adulteration of the end product, causing the fish to be injurious to consumers' health because of bacterial contamination.

In addition to the problem of decomposed and filth-contaminated fish, we have the problem of insanitary [sic] processing and handling procedures which may result in disease in man. Among those most frequently mentioned are botulism, Salmonellosis, and other food poisoning of varying degrees of seriousness.

In 1963, inadequate safeguards in processing smoked lake fish resulted in a major outbreak of botulism; nine persons died. During one weekend in 1966, about 400 cases of salmonella poisoning were reported; the illness was directly attributed to smoked fish. Investigations found unsatisfactory sanitary controls and many sources of contamination in the processing plants.

In 1966, more than 250 cases of food poisoning were reported in one city; imported shrimp was identified as the cause.[20]

The objectives of the Wholesome Fish and Fishery Products Bill are the following:

Developing a comprehensive Federal program for the consumer, protection against the health hazards and mislabeling of fish, shellfish and seafood products.

Setting standards and developing continuous inspection and enforcement.

Supporting research, training and inspection programs.

Helping the States develop their own inspection programs.

Assuring that imported fish and fishery products are wholesome.[21]

Any person who buys fish in an American supermarket today is a gambler. Fish products presently do not receive treatment equal to even the low level of care afforded meat and poultry products. Yet fish is more perishable.

If the Wholesome Fish Bill passes and becomes law someday, fish would receive the same careful inspection that meat and poultry products now receive under the Wholesome Meat Act of 1967, and the consumer will hopefully be able to buy fish products which are graded and inspected at all levels of processing and handling except one. Both the Wholesome Meat Act and the Wholesome Fish Bill are needed to protect the consumer, but in either case the protection stops for the most part when the products reach the unloading docks of the supermarkets.

What good is it to have adequate inspection at every step in the processing and preparation of fish, meats, and poultry if that adequate inspection stops one step before the consumption of the product?

The Food and Drug Administration does not have the manpower to inspect the supermarkets frequently enough to stop the ever increasing rise in food-borne illness.

40 / Meat Eaters are Threatened

Dr. James Goddard, Commissioner of the Food and Drug Administration, has indicated that food poisoning is increasing at an "alarming rate," with Salmonellosis alone increasing more than 1,000 percent since 1951.[22]

Any legislation passed to help curb this increase is welcomed, but the laws should reach into the supermarkets, for when the meat department personnel are lax in the handling of USDA Grade A meat products, previous inspections will give little consolation to the consumer.

CHAPTER III

WHO SAYS THIS STORE ISN'T SAFE?

The Amalgamated Meat Cutter's and Butchers' Workmen's Union and the company supervisors returned me more than once to about 30 of the 60 stores I had worked in to relieve meat managers, first cutters, and journeymen. Because of this unique opportunity, it was easy to notice changes over the years in the areas of health, sanitation, and consumer protection. The changes for the good of the public were negligible in the area of health and sanitation. Manpower has been cut back extensively to help the profit picture. Management has developed little concern for the protection of the consumer. This was particularly evident in a new supermarket in Farmington, Connecticut.

Management bragged openly about the new supermarket's store design, which made it efficient to run and easy to clean. But when I first arrived, I found the first cutter standing in about 2 inches of water in the beef cooler. The water was dripping from the overhead cooler coils. Before the water hit the floor, it passed

Who Says This Store Isn't Safe? / 41

down over permanently installed meat storage racks, coating cube steaks, stew meat, ground beef trimmings, and many other meat items. If the water had become contaminated from bacteria build-up, customers would have found extremely high bacteria counts in their steaks, ground beef, and other meat items, including cold cuts stored for the meat deli. This could present a health hazard. Many stores have this problem. They design the store with no drains in the cooler corner, which also makes it almost impossible to wash the floors properly.

The Kroger Company in some of their new supermarkets in Kansas City, Missouri, has designed the meat department specifically for easy and fast clean-up. There is no sawdust on the cement floors. The floors slope down toward drains, making it easy to clean each night. They have new spraying equipment which they use daily to clean the meat blocks, knife racks, power saws, and grinders. The whole operation is made easy, and all the water runs into the drains. This new concept has saved Kroger money in man-hours, and it gives the public what they should have: equipment free from excessive bacteria build-up.

Another company, which happens to operate exclusively in the East, is doing even a much better job on sanitation. The company is First National. They are using small portable sanitizing machines to clean the entire working area each night. This policy should spread to all of their stores, not just their newer ones. First National has saved money by going to this new clean-up procedure.

Not one of the stores belonging to the chain in which I worked cleaned their power saws, cubing machines, ground beef grinders, knife racks, meat blocks, or any other equipment properly in ten years.

"This Store is Wild"

It was during the summer months. My teaching contract at the University of Hartford had expired, so now I could work vacation relief in other stores. There was a rumor through the grapevine that one of the chains would open a new type of high economy store in the premises of one of their former markets in New Britain, Connecticut. The company had opened a branch in New Jersey, and it was doing so well that they wanted to try one in another area in the East. New Britain was chosen. I had been transferred to the New Britain market before its conversion because one of the journeymen had cut his finger on a highspeed power saw.

While at the Wethersfield store, I had cut my index and middle fingers with a 16-inch steak knife. That was the day before I reported to the New Britain market, so I wasn't in the best condition to work either, but I needed the money.

Before the store was converted, there were three full-time journeymen, the meat manager, and two part-time girls. This was about the right number of personnel for safe working conditions.

The meat manager in this store had a reputation for pushing bad meat. The two journeymen working with me told me to watch the meat manager, that I wouldn't believe the things he does for "gross profit."

Later that afternoon, the meat manager brought in about 5 pounds of slimy, outdated hot dogs, opened them up and threw them in the sink. He indicated that he wanted the hot dogs washed off and repackaged. Later, while I was washing them off, he said, "I have another gift for you." He dumped about 25 pounds of rotten chicken wings in the sink and said, "Do a job on these too." I looked at the guys, and they looked back like "We told you so."

Two days later he pulled out about thirty fully

cooked and smoked hams, half of which were ready to be dumped in the bone barrel. They were rancid, slimy with bacteria, and coated with white and green mold. My job this time was to wash them with cold water and scrub them with a scrub brush. These practices occur daily in supermarkets across the country.

Salmonella could easily be contracted from either the hot dogs or the hams because these items are fully cooked and many people eat them cold. It's easy to see why salmonella has increased 1,000 percent since 1951.

Scores of other abuses took place in the store, but very little shocked me after more than ten years' exposure in the business.

Just How Wild?

I went back to work at the converted new branch on June 28, 1971.

On the way to work that first morning I heard a commercial on a radio station in Hartford. It said, "———— is wild! Prices are sliced to the bone."

When I arrived at the store at 3:30 p.m., there were hundreds of people swarming throughout the store. In the parking lot were five transport trailer trucks with watermelons, meat, dry goods, produce, and groceries. Inside, the walls had been pushed back, making more shelf space. The most noticeable difference was the thousands of food, produce, and meat items stocked on the floor. The chain had a smash, the high-economy store was a success from their standpoint.

The meat department was even more confused and chaotic. There were eleven meat cutters, five supervisors, and seven wrapping girls. Twenty-three meat personnel worked at one time in an area where six had worked previously. The meat cutting room was about 25 feet long and 12 feet wide. And it contained six meat blocks, two power saws, and one 5-foot sink. That cut the working area down to a 20-foot length and a dangerous 5-foot width. Then there was a beef monorail with beef hanging from long hooks, and tree hooks, which took up another 3 or 4 feet, leaving the men just enough room to squeeze through the beef cooler. We had a supervisor working with us in the cutting room at all times, pushing every meat cutter to work faster, faster.

Sometimes three men with 6-inch boning knives and 14-inch steak knives would be working at one 6-foot-long block. The men were never treated well. It was always "Damn it, if you can't get the work out, we can get someone in here who can." We were under constant pressure and intimidation. Many of us received lacerations in the back and arms from the sharp bones and tree hooks behind us. The pace was stepped up even more because the customers were cleaning out the meat case. Trash reached the ceiling and covered most of the work area floor. It was thrown out only when someone fell over it with a knife in his hand. Food trays and meat were all over the cement floor.

The next days were a repeat performance, with still more meat to cut and break down. There were no knife racks to put the knives in, so there were scores of knives scattered over the blocks. I brought out an 85-pound packer round to bone out for top and bottom round roast. There was no way I could see where I was going, and hooks and bones from hanging beef cut into my arms and back as I worked through 60 feet of narrow space to the cutting room. As I dropped the round on the block, a knife flew up in the air about 6 feet and fell next to the beef saw. Since there were no block scrapers, the blocks were slick and slimy with blood, fat, and oil from the joints of the beef. You could spin an 85-pound beef round like a top on the surface of the meat block. Each time I tried to cut the beef, it slipped off the side. Meat was constantly falling on the floor. Sometimes a fallen piece would not be seen until the next day.

The men complained to the supervisors and to each other about the unhealthy and unsafe conditions, but management's reply was, "If you don't like it, get the hell out"; "We're here to make money; when we stop making money, you're going to be out of a job." "You're paid to cut meat, nothing else."

A Little Chicken Water Never Hurt Anyone

The company had not enlarged the meat department, nor had they changed anything except for installing a separate chicken cooler which was especially built to order. It held about a hundred boxes of chickens at one time. It was well constructed but whoever designed it failed to put a drain in it, so there the chicken water and blood, 2 to 3 inches deep, was always running under the door into the meat cooler. Two young boys the store had hired were bagging and cutting chickens all day in this putrid-smelling chicken water.

There were a number of things wrong with this: The Child Labor Act, which is a federal law, was being violated because one of the boys was under eighteen years of age, and he was working near knives and dangerous equipment. The negligence on the part of the store in not providing a chicken drain was unbelievable. The chicken water made it very dangerous to work in the chicken cooler or the chicken-cutting area. Our feet would slip out from under us when we tried to pick up the 100-pound boxes of chickens and ice. Many people working on chickens went crashing onto the cement floor, including me. I finally placed plastic bags over my shoes to keep them dry.

Salmonellosis bacteria develops quite rapidly in chicken water. This water ran into the beef cooler and soaked into thousands of pounds of lunch meat items daily, causing a tremendous potential health problem for the consumer.

Eeny, Meeny, Miny, Mo—Let's Make This Store Really Go!

The store was originally designed to do about $40,000 worth of business a week. The meat department sales figures are almost always about one-fourth of a store's total sales, so they were about $10,000 a week. But this was before the store was converted. Then the store was doing about six times the business it was built to handle. The meat sales were approximately $60,000 a week, which would make the store's total sales approximately $240,000 a week, more than some small companies make in a year.

What Do You Mean, This Store Isn't Safe?

All of the men were complaining about the poor conditions. The morale was quite low, but the supervisors pushed even more. One employee asked, even pleaded to be transferred; he said he couldn't work under the unsafe and unhealthy conditions any longer. The supervisor said, "If you want a job, you have a job—right here—if not, I'm sorry; I can't use you any more." The other employees were told the same thing while the supervisor was in the cutting room. The men told the supervisor they couldn't keep up the pace; someone would be hurt. He replied, "We aren't forcing you to work for us."

After I had been thrown into a power saw because the saw was placed next to a swinging cooler door, it was obvious someone would be hurt seriously very soon. The following letter was signed by eight of the meat cutters working in the store. Their names have been left out because these tradesmen are family men and they must keep their jobs. It's possible they could be blackballed for life from a tradesman position. Most application forms for meat cutting positions include a section asking why you were released from the previous job. If you leave it blank, the company usually finds out by calling the previous employer. This letter is notorized and locked in the safe of the law firm of Kleinman, O'Neil, Steinberg & Lapuk in Hartford, Connecticut, with pictures backing up many of the descriptions in the letter.

The following unsafe conditions exist which may cause bodily injury to any meat department personnel in the near future. "Near future" means a period from a day to several weeks.

There are no knife racks for the meat cutters to place their knives in after use. This creates a real safety hazard to all meat personnel. There are no meat block scrapers to clean the blocks with; consequently, the blocks become very slick from blood and fat which become imbedded on the surface, making it very dangerous to work on. Management has not made adequate safety provisions for the help. Short hooks, long hooks and tree hooks have no mounting rack; thus they must be placed on food racks, causing the possibility of bodily injury either by falling or stabbing the employee. Because of the lack of planning on the part of management, meat storage in the beef cooler, including all hanging beef, veal and lamb, plus box items, take up safety access space for the employees. This makes it very dangerous for employees to go into the cooler to select any meat items for processing. You must crawl through the cooler with barely enough room for your body let alone for the meat or boxes which you must carry.

You must watch out for steel hooks and sharp bones, for either could tear open your face or arm. When you must break down beef, this merely compounds the danger of getting hurt. Trash, fat, meat, bones, wet wrappings from meat and blood all create a danger in both the cooler and the cutting room. Because of management's lack of concern about safety, these items accumulate to the point that it is almost impossible to move from your immediate area without falling.

The cooler doors swing out toward the power saw; thus employees working on the saw could be thrown into the blade, possibly losing either a hand or arm. These and many other unsafe conditions make us feel management does not care about our safety. And we feel it is just a matter of time before someone is seriously hurt.[1]

Two hours after the signing of the letter, one of the meat cutters stabbed himself in the thigh with a 6-inch boning knife. He was rushed into the men's rest room, and an apron was wrapped around the wound to retard the bleeding. He was taken to the hospital. There was a pool of blood left on the floor where he was standing, and several of the employees looked down at it, probably wondering the same thing I did—who would be next? We were told that if the wound had been over just a little to the left, he wouldn't have made it to the hospital alive.

That same day the power saw blade broke, and pieces flew all over the shop like shrapnel, cutting into everything they hit. The same incident happened several times, but management refused to call in a maintenance man. Two weeks later the blade broke again, and pieces struck a meat cutter, just missing his eyes.

What Do You Mean, This Place Isn't Clean?

The meat cutters were equally concerned about poor health and sanitation procedures which affected the public. Seven 55-gallon bone barrels were left outside the store in 80- and 90-degree temperatures for five days, providing a good opportunity to spread disease throughout the New Britain community. The barrels were full of rotten meat, flies and maggots, and the odor was repulsive. Trash and paper wrappings from all meat items, including pork loins, pork butts, hams, and chickens, were thrown out behind the store where dogs, cats, and rodents could drag them off and further threaten the community's health. The trash covered an area of about 80 feet at its base and stretched nearly to the top of the store. There was literally a mountain of rancid trash behind the store. Management didn't seem to think that the bone barrels or the trash presented any real health problem.

Inside, meat was constantly falling on the floor. There wasn't room to stock and store it properly. The floor was covered with sawdust, kitty litter, and fat, making it extremely unsanitary and unsafe.

There was never time to completely clean up the meat shop at night. The power saws, cubing machine, grinder, meat blocks, meat scrapers, and all other equipment were never cleaned properly or daily. Most equipment wasn't cleaned until Saturday of each week.

Mice and rats are a constant menace to supermarkets and meat markets throughout the country. Mice and other rodents were seen during the day and during the night working hours by several employees in the New Britain and in the Wethersfield stores. Accumulation of trash, bone barrels, and other filth can only encourage an increase in rodent population. This is a serious matter, for these rodents can infiltrate a meat department, leaving fecal contamination behind. This contamination can develop coliform bacteria, which in turn breeds disease-causing organisms. This contamination series could develop in ground beef. *Consumer Reports* found that 21 percent of the ground beef samples taken in Philadelphia-area supermarkets showed 100 to 1,000 coliforms per gram, while 52 percent had even higher coliform counts. "Massachusetts ... limits pre-cooked frozen hamburger to only 10 coliforms per gram; the U.S. Public Health Service sets roughly the same limit on pasteurized milk."[2] Los Angeles samples exposed a disgusting fact: the presence of insect fragments and hairs of rodents in hamburger. The report argued that this probably meant fecal contamination, because rodents eat their own hair.[3]

Media & Consumer magazine (July 1973 issue) reprinted some horrifying facts uncovered by Dorothy Brown in an earlier article in the *Philadelphia Bulletin* in 1973. The title of the article, "Philadelphia Supermarkets: The Beginning of a National Scandal" should be enough to alarm most people, but when you start to read the article, you start to get mad. "Excessively high bacteria levels were found in 12 out of 12 raw hamburger samples purchased at random." None of the samples tested fall safely below the 100 (Coliform bacteria count) per gram level that is considered acceptable by most food technologists.

While in the Wethersfield market one day, the meat inspector just missed seeing several large mice running under the conveyor line. While the inspector's back was turned, a meat cutter ran over to the sink and drowned a large mouse by holding it under water.

The following letter was signed by seven of the eleven meat cutters working at a market in New Britain.

> The following conditions exist which are against local and state laws concerning health and sanitation. There is a special chicken cooler which

was recently built for storing chickens. This cooler does not have a drain in it; consequently, blood, chicken water and bacteria are allowed to build up. This cooler has not been cleaned for seven days to date. Bone barrels full of fat, rotten meat, bones and blood are stored outside the building in temperatures of 80 or 90 degrees, thus causing a potential health hazard to the community. This creates a breeding place for flies and other pests. There is also danger of bacteria and disease being spread by rats and other rodents which are found in the area. Trash from all departments is being thrown out against the building, and at times it reaches nearly to the top of the structure. All meat department wrappings from reworks, and unwrappings from pork loins, butts, hams, and chickens are also found in the trash at all times. This draws flies and other pests and could cause a health problem for the city. The equipment used for processing all meat, including power saws, ground beef grinder, cubing machine, meat scrapers, hand saws, meat blocks and knives, are not cleaned properly. It seems management does not care about clean-up. Production takes up all the time. This lack of concern about health and sanitation puts both the meat cutters and the public at a disadvantage.

Because of inadequate storage room, fresh meat is sometimes stored on top of boxes or anything else you can find, so meat is constantly falling on the floor.

We feel the company is remiss in its obligation to the consumer, for health and sanitation should be the first and foremost concern of any company involved in the processing and preparation of any food products.[4]

Section 19-13B40 of the Public Health Code of the State of Connecticut states:

> No person, firm or corporation shall sell, offer for sale or keep for sale any groceries, bakery products, confectioneries, meats, fish, vegetables or fruits except after compliance with the following requirements: [Part A] All food and drink shall be clean, wholesome, free from spoilage and so prepared as to be safe for human consumption. All food and drink shall be so stored, displayed and served as to be protected from dust, flies, vermin, depredation and pollution by rodents, unnecessary handling, droplet infection, overhead leakage or other contamination. No animals or fowls shall be kept or allowed in any room in which food or drink is prepared or stored. All means necessary for the elimination of flies, roaches and rodents shall be used. All exposed food shall be stored at least eighteen inches above the floor and all food which may be contaminated by exposure when deposited at a food establishment on delivery shall be stored at least eighteen inches above the floor. Food cooking or processing operations shall be conducted in a sanitary manner.[5]

The Connecticut Public Health Code was violated by a national chain store by having fowl processed in an unrefrigerated cutting area. The code was further violated by having cut-up and bagged chickens left in grocery carts out of refrigeration for several hours. On several occasions chickens were pushed out on the loading dock, where they sat for several hours in 90-degree temperatures. Flies and rodents were present. A & P violated the code also by placing cold cuts and other precooked meats directly on the floor, thus exposing these items to potential insect infestation and bacteria contamination from chicken water and blood seepage.

In the Wethersfield market, hot roast beefs that vary in length from 10 to 18 inches are taken directly out of the "deli oven" and put into the meat department, where they are placed on aluminum meat trays and pushed down a conveyor line for a distance of 50 feet. The pans are almost always contaminated with pieces of rancid meat left over from months of neglected clean-up. The walls may be cleaned only once every six months to a year, so meat passing down the length of the conveyor picks up bacteria contamination when it scrapes the wall.

Rotten meat, including pork chops, spare ribs, chickens, and country ribs, are usually taken to the deli for barbecue preparation. After being cooked, they are placed on the same filthy meat trays and exposed to still more bacteria contamination.

Part B of the Connecticut Health Code states:

> The floor, walls, windows and ceilings of rooms used for preparation and sale of foods shall be kept clean and in good repair.[6]

This chain does not abide by this section of the health code. Holding or back-up storage coolers in the Wethersfield store had not been cleaned for six months.

Floors, walls, windows, and ceilings in meat markets get extremely filthy from blood, water, fat, and decomposed meat. Power saws throw small pieces of meat, bone, and fat in all directions, bombarding all surfaces with flying debris. Grinding machines have spewed meat for distances of 15 feet, throwing fat and meat all over the walls, ceiling, and floor. Nevertheless, walls are rarely cleaned, and this is also true of windows and ceilings, not to mention the sawdust and kitty litter. Floors are swept, *but in the past ten years, in all the twenty large stores of this chain I have worked in, I have not seen one floor in any of the meat departments cleaned with cleaning solution and water.*

Packing houses clean and wash their floors each night. Why not supermarkets?

Part C of the Connecticut Health Code reads:

> All equipment shall be so installed and maintained as to facilitate the cleaning thereof, and of all adjacent areas. All equipment and utensils shall be kept clean.[7]

At least once a day machines such as power saws, grinders and cubing machines should be taken apart and cleaned with cleaning solution and water or sprayed with steam. The machines in the stores I worked in are not taken apart and cleaned properly any more often than once every week.

On many occasions ground beef grinders are allowed to go for a month without cleaning. This neglect causes a tremendously high bacteria count in all ground meats, even though these machines are usually under some refrigeration.

Part D of the Connecticut Health Code states:

> Any food to be eaten without cooking shall not be stored directly in contact with ice. All refrigerators shall be kept in a clean and sanitary condition. All potentially hazardous food which consists in whole or in part of milk or milk products, eggs, meat, poultry, fish, shellfish, or other ingredients capable of supporting the rapid and progressive growth of infectious or toxigenic micro-organisms, shall be maintained at safe temperatures at 45°F. or below, or 140°F. or above, except during necessary periods of preparation.[8]

Who Says This Store Isn't Safe? / 55

Ready-to-consume precooked lunch meats and deli items are usually stored in the meat department coolers. This is where they come in contact with ice and water from the chickens stored next to these items.

Part G of the Connecticut Health Code states:

> No decayed fruits, meats, fish, vegetables or other foods shall be allowed to remain in any receptacle where in any fruits, meats, fish, vegetables or other foods intended for human consumption are kept for sale or other disposition. All garbage and rubbish containing food wastes shall, prior to disposal, be kept in a leak-proof, non-absorbent container which shall be kept covered with tight fitting lids when filled or stored, or not in continuous use; (provided such containers need not be covered when stored) in a vermin-proofed room or enclosure, or in a food waste refrigerator. All other rubbish shall be stored in containers, rooms or areas in an approved manner. The rooms, enclosures, areas and containers used shall be adequate for the storage of all food waste and rubbish accumulating on the premises.[9]

Bone barrels were left outside of refrigeration behind the store, and they were not covered. There were no trash receptacles; trash blew all over the parking lot, and at times it reached nearly to the top of the building.

Part I of the Connecticut Health Code states:

> Each establishment shall be provided with adequate, conveniently located toilet facilities for its employees. Toilet facilities, including rooms and fixtures, shall be sanitary and readily cleaned and shall be kept in a clean condition and in good repair.[10]

Part J of the Connecticut Code states:

> All parts of the establishment and its premises shall be kept neat, clean and free of litter and rubbish. Cleaning operations shall be conducted in such a manner as to minimize contamination of food and food contact surfaces.[11]

The public health standards described by the Public Health Code are guidelines for the protection of the public. Unfortunately, these health standards are not being followed by the retail supermarkets. A good example of this is given in an Associated Press release dated February 28, 1973. A large chain store on Route 37 in Toms River, New Jersey, was ordered closed on February 28, 1973. Numerous roaches were found living in the walls and ceiling of the basement food storage area. According to the State Health Department, "The store's meat grinder was encrusted with heavy, black malodorous debris." The meat saw was also reported dirty, with encrusted old meat coating its surface. Urinals in the men's toilet were clogged and were emitting foul odors. Both the women's and the men's toilets were stained with fecal material. All the hand-washing sinks were stained and soiled, and it was also noted that frozen food cases were filthy. Hats off to the New Jersey Health Department, but don't think for one minute that this is an isolated case. The only thing unusual about this case was the fact that this time, after repeated warnings to the store, the state did finally close the store.

If you were to visit the rest room of your local supermarket before making your purchase at the meat deli or meat department, perhaps there would be no purchase. The best way to envision the conditions of the average supermarket rest room is to close your eyes and think of some of the busy, busy gas station rest rooms you had to use of necessity on a recent trip. But remember, gas station attendants don't process and handle food items for public consumption.

This chain has not implemented any consistent program to comply with the Connecticut Public Health Code.

Raw Pork Won't Hurt You, Much!

Supervisory personnel perpetrate even more serious abuses which can harm and even kill. One of these is the deliberate adulteration of ground beef.

On July 3, 1971, a meat supervisor ordered a meat cutter to put pork and veal into the ground beef grind in a large market in New Britain, Connecticut. This is one of the easiest ways to adulterate ground beef. When the company has large amounts of veal and pork trimmings, they mix it into the beef trimmings as they grind. State inspectors cannot check this type of adulteration on the premises. Their on-the-spot checks merely show if nitrates were introduced and indicate the fat-to-lean content. They do not differentiate between pork and beef. Determining this would require extensive lab analysis. *Consumer Reports*, July 1973: From "The Docket"—"The Great Atlantic & Pacific Tea Co., Inc.—operator of A&P supermarkets—was ordered by the Milwaukee County Circuit Court not to sell adulterated meat in violation of Wisconsin statutes. That state's Attorney General filed a complaint in the circuit court charging that A&P intentionally added pork to meat labeled as being fresh ground beef. The Attorney General said that A&P had pleaded guilty on numerous occasions to offering adulterated meat for sale and he alleged that the company would continue to adulterate meat because of inadequate penalties provided for in the state statutes."

In 1957 the World Health Organization estimated that trichinosis was more prevalent in the United States than in any other part of the world. Although the incidence of trichinosis from pork has gradually declined in the United States over the past twenty years, there will be a reversal if the trend of mixing pork in ground beef continues to gain popularity. The reason why companies put pork and veal into their ground beef is to use up "product overage" which otherwise may have to be thrown away. By using the "product overage" in the ground beef, the stores avoid throwing it away and increase their gross profits. Any meat cutter will confirm the fact that very few things are ever thrown away, especially not fresh pork overage.

If the ground beef is eaten rare or raw, as many people eat it, trichinosis may be contracted. Trichinosis is a parasitic infection of man and animals caused by a nematode (worm), *Trichinella spiralis*. The usual mode of infection in man is through eating infected pork which has been inadequately cooked or treated. The parasites are referred to as trichina worms. In the small intestine larvae develop to a mature adult stage; then they mate. This maturity takes only a few hours and the mating usually takes place within two or three days. The male worm is finally passed out of the body, but the female worms pass larvae into the intestinal wall. From there the larvae invade the lymphatic and are disseminated through the blood stream to the heart. Then they are pushed throughout the body and only the muscle tissue will provide an adequate environment for further development.

Trichinosis symptoms include diarrhea, nausea, and vomiting, usually within two to four days, after consumption of the infected meat, especially if there was a large number of larvae in the meat. Usually there will be a swelling of the upper eyelids. Muscle soreness and pain along with skin lesions, thirst, profuse sweating, chills, weakness, headaches, and fever may also occur. Some individuals even shy away from light because of eye pain and eye hemorrhage. If the worms attack the heart, nerves or the respiratory system death may result.[12]

The average number of cases reported over the past twenty-one years was 267 cases per year. The National Communicable Disease Center in Atlanta, Georgia, reported that there were only 67 reported cases of trichinosis in 1967.[13]

The *Federal Register* goes to great length explaining why and how pork and pork products must be treated to kill trichina worms. Products made with pork especially might be consumed without proper cooking in the home. Such products include bologna, frankfurters, viennas, smoked sausage, knoblauch sausage, mortadella, smoked hams, and all cold cuts and lunch meat items.

The United States government considers that trichina worm destruction should consist of heating, refrigerating, or curing under strict rules and guidelines relating to temperatures, thickness of the meat and duration of treatment.[14]

However, none of the fresh pork received from processing plants receives this treatment because it is assumed that the consumer knows that all fresh pork items must be fully cooked and never eaten rare or raw.

On January 19, 1967, six days after eating two raw meat sandwiches, a thirty-nine-year-old man in Seattle, Washington, became quite ill. He experienced fever, nausea, diarrhea, malaise, and diffuse muscle pain. Fifteen days after this onset, he was taken to the hospital and found to have muscle tenderness, dyplopia and puffy eyelids. The white blood cell counts varied. On February 7 they gave him a muscle biopsy and diagnosed his case as *Trichinella spiralis* infection.

While at home on January 12, 1967, the patient had prepared and eaten two sandwiches made of rare ground beef. He states that he had developed a taste for raw meat while working as a butcher. He thought the meat was pure beef, but later found that his wife had mixed a pound of pork sausage with 2 pounds of ground beef for a special dish she was making.

The pork sausage that the wife mixed with the beef had been processed by a neighborhood market from pork loin trimmings and shoulder trimmings. Since the market received pork from a number of sources, it was impossible to determine the farm source.

The manager of the meat market indicated that he usually tasted bits of raw sausage while preparing it to see if it was seasoned properly. He denied any past illness suggestive of trichinosis, but a test later showed that he had contracted the disease.

You Can't Take Pictures in a Meat Market

On July 3, 1971, I took pictures of local, state and federal violations of health, sanitation and safety laws in the supermarket branch store in New Britain, Connecticut. I managed to get 24 pictures to document the letters signed earlier by market employees. There were many pictures I could not take because supervisors were present.

While I was cutting chickens in an unrefrigerated cutting area, a late-model green Chevrolet pulled up to the back door of the meat department. A meat cutter got out of the car, opened the trunk, and asked me to help him unload some beef plates which were to be boned out for ground beef. I took two color pictures of the meat, which had been carried in a 90-degree temperature in the trunk of the car for a distance of about 25 miles. Such transportation violates federal and state laws and presents a clear and present danger to the consuming public. There were four similar shipments in old and new cars that day. A dark green Plymouth brought in precooked lunch meat items from the Wethersfield market. The meat, later to be eaten by unsuspecting customers, had flies, dirt, and grease from the tire tools covering the surfaces.

The meat cutters did not leave their jobs at another store without being specifically ordered to do so by the meat supervisors.

The state and local agencies including city health departments and state consumer protection divisions must put a stop to this and similar acts being perpetrated against the American public.

Saturdays are important to the profit picture, for if too much meat is cut, it must be reworked on Monday morning. Reworks cost the company money.

One Saturday I suggested to a supervisor that if we dated our beef trimmings, we could give the customers a fresher product free from bacterial contamination, and the company would enhance their gross profit by cutting down shrinkage and product putrefaction. He said it would take too much time to date the beef pans; anyway, the pans were moving fast enough. As I turned around to look into the cutting room, I noticed that about six of approximately twenty beef trimming pans had rotten meat in them. I said, "This is what I mean. Would you want to eat ground beef made from rancid trimmings?" When I turned around, he was gone; the other supervisor had called him to discuss something. I noticed that all the old pork, veal and dark steaks which wouldn't make it to Monday morning had been placed in the ground beef grinder for final grind. This is a good way to clean up on a few items you can't sell. Camouflage them in about 50 pounds of beef trimmings; then grind them—no one will ever know. I was about 40 feet away from my camera, but it seemed like a mile because supervisors were everywhere.

I finished hanging some chucks on a tree hook, and they said to bring them into the cutting room. We

62 / Meat Eaters are Threatened

needed several more to get through the night. I knew that the supervisor was working on one of the power saws, and if I could just push the chucks out and use them for cover, I could reach my camera without being seen. All the meat cutters knew what I was doing, and they helped me whenever they could. They would even warn me if a supervisor was coming. I grabbed my camera from under the meat block and went back into the beef cooler to take a shot of the adulteration of ground beef. On the first picture the flash didn't work. I took the flash cube off to check it, and a meat cutter said, "Watch out, the old man is on his way." I told him I had to get a shot I'd been trying to get for months, but on every occasion by the time I got my camera out of my car or from some other place, the evidence was gone. He said, "I know what you mean, but hurry up." It was too late; just as I started to take the picture, the meat supervisor walked in on me. He said, "What in the hell do you think you're doing? You can't take pictures back here. Get that camera out of here right now. Don't you know it's against company policy to take pictures in a meat department without permission? I don't want you taking any more pictures." I put the camera away; I couldn't use it anyway because my battery was dead.

After I finished working Saturday night, I checked the schedule for the next week and noticed that someone had drawn a black line through my name and hours. The meat manager said, "Oh, that was a mistake, someone marked through it by accident." I thought maybe they had fired me without my knowing it, but no such luck.

Monday morning I came back to work thirty minutes early with some new batteries to get a few shots of the seven bone barrels which had sat out in 80- and 90-degree temperatures for five days. I had taken pictures each day to document the letter signed by the meat cutters. A union official was looking at the barrels, full of rotten meat, fat, flies, and maggots, which covered the meat like a white sheet. The men were insisting to the union official that the conditions must stop. I observed the incident from the side of the building. After the loading door was closed, I took four shots, two wide-angle and two close-ups. I put my meat smock and apron on and had started to walk into the meat cutting room when the head meat supervisor stopped me and said, "Wait a minute, fellow; we want to talk to you." There were five men standing around in suits, and it looked very official.

They took me out to the parking lot. The union official was there, along with the company personnel manager from Springfield, Massachusetts. The head supervisor started the conversation: "I understand you've been taking pictures. Just who do you think you are? Don't you know it's against company policy to take pictures in a meat department without permission? Don't you know these are grounds for dismissal?" I told him I had never seen it in writing; besides, there was an issue that was far more important than concern over taking pictures in a meat department; namely, consumer protection. The union official said there was no question about my work; the reason the meeting was called was because it's against company policy to take pictures without permission. I asked why it was against company policy to take pictures in a meat department. Could this practice be detrimental to the community or the national security? No one gave me an answer. Instead, the head supervisor said, "It's our opinion you have violated company policy—you're fired!"

I later asked the union official what he had to say. He replied, "The union hasn't had their say yet." Two meat cutters came out—very carefully, so they wouldn't be seen by the supervisors—to talk to the union official. They covered up their presence by carrying out trash, so it would look legitimate. They said, "This guy's 100 percent right; you had better fight for him." They were afraid because the company has ways of making it rough for a man who causes waves.

I walked through the meat cutting room with the union official, pointing out conditions that affected the men's safety and the public's health. Three medium- and the bags were lying empty outside the cooler door. Some chickens were lying in the kitty litter. size bags of kitty litter had been dumped on the floor,

As I pointed out the conditions, the supervisor agreed in the presence of the union official that these conditions should be rectified. The supervisor overheard me say that the state would be brought in the next day. The men were ordered to sweep up the kitty litter immediately. When we came back through the cutting room again, it was gone, leaving only a dust cover in its place. The chickens had been picked up off the floor. I had informed the state officials, but by the time they would arrive, the meat department would be in good order. Several of the men called me afterward and said the store brought in crews to straighten the situation out before the state official came.

The personnel manager told me I had to sign a release form. I read the form and refused to sign it unless I could indicate the real reason I was fired. I wrote on the back of the form: "I was released because I was documenting unsafe conditions perpetrated against the employees and unhealthy and unsanitary practices perpetrated against the consuming public."

This form was probably destroyed along with other evidence involving the case. But the facts remain—the chain had done the American public a real disservice despite any bargains in price.

The State Consumer Protection Division found the store in violation of several regulations, even though the market had prepared for the inspection. The State

Industrial Safety Division also found several violations. The state inspector who made the safety report called me.

He said, "They were ready for me when I arrived. They were just finishing installation of the knife guards on the blocks." They were in violation of many safety regulations.

Mr. Kenneth Crain, chief of the Food, Drug, Meat and Poultry Inspection for the state said, "The conditions at ———— were pretty much the same as described in the letter dated July 3, 1971." I was surprised that the state found anything, because the employees documented in sworn testimony before my lawyer that the store had made many changes right after I was fired.

The conditions which exist in many supermarkets owned and operated by this company and other companies have continued to get progressively worse over the last ten years. The hands of consumer protection agencies are tied—present legislation does not give them the manpower or the authority to act.

CHAPTER IV

THE APPRENTICESHIP

To see whether there has been any change in the retail meat business, I must go back ten years to 1961, when I started out as an apprentice in Missouri and Kansas.

The apprentice program for a meat cutter lasts two years. As your apprenticeship progresses, you go through various stages, starting off with the chores of carrying out trash, cutting up and packing chickens, and weighing, pricing, and grinding beef. You very seldom pick up a knife, at least not until the first six-month period has elapsed. Then you begin to trim steaks and break beef. By this time, you have become familiar with the various cuts of meat so when you are told to get a round of beef, you don't go in and pick up a loin by mistake, or, when they tell you to pull out a tree of flanks, you don't go in and pull out a tree of plates. By this time you have learned to tell the difference between flanks, plates, loins, and rounds.

Eventually you become proficient at cutting lamb, veal and pork, and finally beef. You are aware of the total processing of beef—not just breaking down the beef into various cuts like the stripping of the flank from the hindquarter or taking out the tip and separating the round from the loin. This takes both strength and some degree of talent. But the real talent shows when you are able to take these various cuts and "final process" them—cut them into bone-in steaks, roasts, and filets. This is the true art of meat cutting. It takes sixteen months of apprenticeship to reach that point.

The last eight months are devoted to heavy cutting on the power saw and checking your proficiency in all meat areas, including poultry, fish, lamb, veal, pork, and beef. You learn how to get the most profit out of each item. You learn how to merchandise all meat items. Then you are transferred to another store to finish your apprenticeship. In this way, you find out other methods of doing the same job. It is a good idea.

I was working for one of America's largest supermarket chains. After working in ten other of their stores, they decided to terminate five apprentices and four journeymen because business was slow. I was in that group.

An independent food chain offered me a temporary job, and I took it immediately. The store was new and had all the latest equipment. I was started on chickens, bagging them outside the store for a sale. This is a usual practice for some companies in chicken sales; it is easier to do the bagging outside the store for several reasons: Labor is saved because the trash doesn't have to be carried outside; and the cooler is kept free of the chicken water and melting ice that flow freely from the large number of boxes. This practice benefits the company, but it harms the consumer. The temperatures in the summer heat I was working in cause a very rapid incubation of bacteria, decreasing the chances that the consumer will get a fresh product.

You Just Caught the "Bug"—That's All, Honey

The meat deli was just a catchall for all the bad meat we couldn't sell. If we had dark ground beef, it went to the meat deli, where they turned it into meat loaf. Nothing was thrown out. Chickens that were brought back by customers for refunds because they were rotten were rushed over to the deli to be prepared as barbecued chicken or sometimes chicken salad. Any old meat that was left over was always mixed into some kind of meat dish or salad.

When we had ends and pieces left over from the cold cuts, we would place them on a tray in the back of the room until there was a sufficient amount to slice on the slicing machine. These cold cuts were sold at a reduced price, but anyone eating sandwiches made from this bargain was playing with death. On many occasions these cold cuts would go for three or four weeks before they were sliced. The meat was slick from the bacteria build-up.

Chickens were left out of refrigeration after being cooked. Sometimes they would go for weeks before someone would buy them. They were always placed in a warmer, but this consisted only of a couple of small lights that maintained a temperature of about 90 degrees—actually increasing the opportunity for bacteria incubation.

Chickens are highly susceptible to salmonella organisms. This bacteria is named after Dr. D. E. Salmon, an American veterinarian, who found that the bacteria affects the intestinal tract and tissues of humans.[1] The resulting symptoms are fever, diarrhea, abdominal cramps, and sometimes vomiting. The effects vary from diarrhea to death. Health officials feel that there may be 2 million cases a year, but the great majority of cases are diagnosed as a "virus" or the flu.[2] This is also true of other types of food poisoning. In many cases the patient doesn't even call the doctor. Many times the illness ends after vomiting or cramps. Later, the person will blame it on indigestion or having eaten too fast.

As mentioned in Chapter II, about 400 cases of salmonella poisoning were repored during one weekend in 1966; in this incident, the illness was directly attributable to smoked fish.

It's time to stop playing games with our bodies. Former Food and Drug Administration Commissioner Dr. James Goddard argued:

> Salmonella has become a major public health problem which is continually increasing in complexity. Despite new sanitary procedures for manufacturing, handling, storing, preparing and serving food, the incidence of the disease is rising throughout the world.[3]

Dr. Goddard indicated that cattle and hogs are considered major sources of salmonella infection. Meat chosen at random in retail markets showed a high incidence of contamination. This is particularly true of pork products. "A study in Florida revealed that salmonella contamination of fresh sausage and pork ranged from 8 percent in samples from national distributors to 58 percent from local abattoirs."[4]

Rats, mice, and insects can also carry salmonella into food, and all of these pests are found in and around most supermarkets.

Dr. Oscar Sussman, chief of the Veterinary Public Health program for New Jersey, stated:

> No present method of U.S. meat or poultry inspection can assure disease-free, non-contaminated raw meat or poultry products. Reliance by the housewife on the U.S. Inspected legend alone has, can, and will cause countless cases of food infection such as salmonella and trichinosis.[5]

Dr. Sussman was warning the consumer against becoming lazy and lax in the handling, preparing, and checking of all meat items. A USDA stamp on the meat doesn't prevent bacteria formation. If the food is cooked thoroughly, the bacteria will be killed, but in the case of deli items ready to be eaten without cooking, the consumer is in real danger. According to the Center for Disease Control in Atlanta, Georgia, there were 19,740 reported cases of salmonella poisoning in 1968. In 1969, the number of reported cases increased 22.7 percent to 21,413 cases. In 1970, there was another rise of 13.1 percent, bringing the total reported cases of salmonella poisoning to 24,216 cases.[6] How many other cases of salmonella were not reported because they were mistaken for something else?

This was about the time of the botulism scare in Detroit, Michigan, which occurred because of contaminated tuna which had been shipped in frozen from Japan, and later canned by the Dagimtashorin Brand Tuna in California. Earlier, in 1964, *Consumer Reports* had said, "By far the best tuna fish is packed by the Japanese, who fish off the same waters our packers use,

70 / Meat Eaters are Threatened

but who pack their tuna in a different way—aboard ship, so that it is far juicier and meatier than our brands."[7]

Three women got together for lunch; they were having homemade tuna fish salad. One of the women mentioned that she thought the tuna had a funny smell, but then the other women tasted it, and they decided it was all right. So all three women ate some tuna fish. Later, around dinner time, one of the women complained to her husband about blurred vision. She constantly put her glasses on and took them off. She went to bed without supper and later complained about difficulty in breathing. As in most cases of food poisoning, both she and her husband thought she was coming down with the flu.

Early the next morning her husband was awakened by his wife's very heavy, convulsive breathing. Her voice was constrained. An emergency unit rushed her to the hospital but it was too late—she was dead on arrival.

One of her companions by that time had begun to suffer from symptoms of dizziness, blurred vision and difficult breathing. Later, she started vomiting and became uncoordinated in her movements. Both she and her husband misdiagnosed the sickness as the flu until they heard about her friend's death. The woman was taken to the hospital, where she was given polyvalent Type A and B botulinus antitoxin. There was no improvement, so Type E antitoxin was given four days later, with still no change detectable. She died. Only one of the three women pulled through. Given A and B polyvalent botulinus antitoxin, she recovered after three days of treatment.[8]

Although this was apparently an isolated case, death from botulism seems to worry many people. In this case, it was suspected that the bacteria entered the can through faulty seams.

The year 1971 saw three isolated botulism scares, one in New Jersey, one in Texas, and one in California.

There is constant danger of staph-ptomaine poisoning from the improper health and sanitation procedures in meat delis in the United States. This food poisoning may be more prevalent than salmonella; however, it is rarely fatal—and probably also rarely recognized as food poisoning. The disease stems from the staphylococcus germ, which is carried by human beings on the skin, in the throat, and on wounds which are infected. Foods such as sliced meats, salads, and puddings, which are directly handled by people preparing them, are therefore almost unavoidably contaminated with some staph germs. If the store is negligent with these foods, failing to keep them cool or transporting them in a hot car from store to store, toxins start to grow at a tremendous rate. If such foods are taken on a day's outing to the beach, and the consumer fails to keep them cool, the chances are even greater for a serious case of staph poisoning.

The incubation period for staph poisoning takes place within two to four hours after eating. The symptoms start quickly with queasiness and vomiting. The nausea lasts from three to six hours, but the illness is rarely fatal.

Cold cuts, processed meat and fish, custards, cream-filled bakery items, and milk, which are found often in meat delicatessens, are all highly susceptible to staph poisoning.

Shigella is another bacterial disease, often referred to as bacillary dysentery, which can easily be transferred through meat department delicatessens. If flies and rodents, the main carriers of shigella are present during the working hours, think how many pests come out during the night to infect the meats, salads, and desserts while there was no one present.

Mice and other rodents have a way of getting into meat storage rooms and cutting rooms, and even the new supermarkets are plagued by the pests.

Dysentery can be a serious disease, especially in the case of infant children and elderly or debilitated persons. The incubation period is from one to seven days, usually less than four days in most cases. The length of this period makes it difficult to find the suspected food.

The symptoms include diarrhea, fever, and often vomiting and cramps.[9] The disease was widespread across the United States the year I was working in this and many other meat departments.

Meat delicatessens are guilty of mishandling many precooked and ready-to-eat dishes; such mishandling can result in another common food poisoning caused by the bacterium *Clostridium perfringens*. This disease is an intestinal disorder characterized by colic-like cramps, diarrhea, and nausea. The disease is usually mild, lasting about one day, and for this reason most cases go unreported. The majority of cases are associated with meat dishes, stews, reheated meats, and gravies made with chicken, turkey, or beef.[10] Meat delis reheat dishes for days, never throwing anything out, just adding to it each day. This practice creates a good medium for this disease.

The United States Public Health Service, in a report issued over ten years ago, recommended "a five-to-six-fold increase in the scope and intensity of both the intramural and extramural food-protection activities of the Public Health Service."[11] The report also recommended that "positive action is needed to stem the trend toward obsolescence of the food protection program in public health agencies, and thus keep pace with the developments in food science and technology. In contrast to the notable progress made in food sanitation during the first half of the 20th century, this area of government activity has now become the weakest link in the protection of the nation's food supply."[12] Perhaps the best way to stop the increase of food poisoning in the United States is to expose the inherent risks involved in the preparation and handling of food through compulsory education courses for all food handlers.

This Stuff Is "Dynamite"

Food poisoning wasn't the only potential danger related to this meat department. One day for about two hours the meat manager had me painting steaks with a 5-inch brush as they rolled past on a conveyor line. The solution, a compound mixed with water in a 2-gallon bucket, was unknown to me. It seemed like an easy job compared to my usual chores; apprentices are usually given the worst detail. I continued painting everything that came down the line, including all beef and pork items. Later, a young journeyman told me the meat manager put "dynamite" in almost every piece of meat that was processed. The term "dynamite" was trade talk for sodium sulphite, which is a powerful chemical that holds the color of the meat.

This chemical is poison, and it is illegal to use in meats, but some meat markets use it, especially when they are having gross profit difficulty.

The meat managers claim that sodium sulphite is a safe preservative, but the government says it is not. Besides being a poison itself, sodium sulphite creates another danger when it is used—though it gives the meat a bright color on the surface, the meat on the inside could be green.

The ground meats like chuck, round, sirloin, and sausage are even more dangerous, because the sulphite solution is mixed in the grind by hand first, then run through a grinder, which mixes it evenly. You may buy some ground beef that is heavily contaminated with bacteria, but you won't know it because the so-

74 / **Meat Eaters are Threatened**

dium sulphite hides the bad odor and keeps the meat's red appearance. If meat appears extremely bright red in the case of beef items, you may be right in assuming that it has been adulterated.

Not too many years ago the State Food Commissioner of Connecticut warned meat departments that if the fast-growing practice of putting sulphite into hamburger to hide decomposition continued, prosecution would result.

This warning must have done some good, for the 1966 through 1970 issues of the Bulletin of the Connecticut Agricultural Experiment Station in New Haven showed little evidence of adulteration through the use of sulphites. Mr. Eaton E. Smith, director of the Food and Drug Division in the Consumer Protection Division of Connecticut, indicated that very little evidence was found of any meat markets using sulphites. Perhaps other states should follow suit by making strong statements that can be backed up. Sulphites can kill when used in excess.

We're Number Three, But We Try Harder

After being hired by a second national chain in 1963, I continued my college education in night school while working full-time in the meat business during the day.

Everything I was learning on the job was for the benefit of "G.P."—Mr. Gross Profit. The head meat cutter would say:

> When you trim, scrape, and tray this roast, keep in mind that it must sell. Don't put this side up: Would you buy that roast if you saw that large bone? Turn it over; display it so it has "consumer appeal." Don't trim that ham fat off like that; trim it at an angle so it looks like you have taken off

the same amount. See, it looks good, doesn't it? Don't place those end-cut pork chops on top; bury them. Would you buy that package if you saw those chops on top? Hide the bad ones!

It takes a wild imagination—or ESP—for the customer to figure out what surprises she will find inside her packaged meat.

Each store seems about the same, as I was then beginning to realize; there is little difference between various companies. When it comes to gross profit, to hell with consumer fair practices, to hell with clean-up, to hell with treating your help like human beings.

I was, however, surprised that this company at certain periods of time would have a big push on daily clean-up: cleaning the shop every night, cleaning the blocks and underneath them, cleaning the saws, cleaning the conveyor line, cleaning the entire working and cutting area, and even the meat coolers and chicken troughs. Usually management would permit a clean-up push only once a year.

The district man for the company came through the meat cutting room door and walked up to the head meat cutter, saying, "Why haven't you cleaned up this market?" The head meat cutter was naturally behind in clean-up. With a grin on his face, the district man said at the top of his voice, "Dave, this place is a filthy, goddamn mess—bacteria on this block and underneath it—breeding! If you don't clean it up, you're going to get yourself in a lot of trouble." The head meat cutter's light-hearted rebuttal was, "You mean I'm up here on this meat block working like a son-of-a-bitch for you and those little bastards are underneath my feet breeding." Humor was a reflection of the confusion that arose from the company's sudden decision to clean up. All the company had ever placed emphasis on before was production: Everyone had been trained to realize that clean-up doesn't make money. People just can't re-gear their thinking in a few days after being indoctrinated for years to think that health and sanitation are last on the list.

Most states prescribe that ground beef must not have over a certain amount of fat content. Many states are trying to pattern their rules and regulations for meat inspection after the federal government's guidelines described in the Federal Register, Department of Agriculture Wholesome Meat Act. From the Federal Register Sub-part B—Raw Meat Products, the following requirements for ground beef are as follows:

> "Chopped Beef" or "Ground Beef" shall consist of chopped fresh and/or frozen beef with or without seasoning and without the addition of beef fat as such, shall not contain more than 30 percent fat, and shall not contain added water, binders, or extenders.[13]

For some reason, when we put ground beef on sale, the store just couldn't quite stick to those state and federal requirements. The word around the market on that day might be "Push the fat" and that was what we did—we pushed the fat. One grind in particular was almost as white as a piece of typing paper, and the big joke around the market was: "Wait, it'll bloom. Just let it sit on the conveyor line long enough and it will turn red." We waited and waited but it didn't turn red. It didn't quite bloom, but we put it out in the meat case and some unsuspecting customers bought it. I can only estimate that the fat content in that ground beef was somewere around 65 percent, which most certainly is far beyond the limits of the state and federal laws.

It was at this market that I became aware of the adulteration of ground beef with pork. I became aware also that this practice was followed in a great many other markets, and I have already described in Chapter III the similar practices I saw later.

When this market became overstocked with pork trimmings, they would be put into the ground beef. We couldn't grind enough of it into sausage. When the ground beef sale came, we just mixed a little bit of pork in with a little bit of beef. The store couldn't throw it away—that's "gross profit."

Fresh pork should be fully cooked before eating. It should not be put into ground beef to save the company's gross profit. As mentioned in Chapter III, the *Federal Register* states quite clearly that only fresh beef can be added to ground beef. The *Federal Register* goes into great detail in prescribing the treatment of pork and products containing pork to destroy trichina worms. The particular adulteration I witnessed took place in Missouri in 1964, but the same conditions exist today in Kansas, Connecticut, and Missouri.

One of the most disgusting practices I witnessed was the buying of cod fat and suet from the bone man when the company ran low on beef trimmings. This fat was almost always covered with maggots and other insects. There was also the danger of fecal contamination from rats, as many of the bone barrels were left outside in the summer heat.

The Independent Food Store

The company had not given me a schedule during my term break from college. I was listed with the Amalgamated Meat Cutter's and Butcher's Workmen's Union, and an independent store in northern Missouri found that I was available. I decided to work for them.

I had worked in many small independent stores, but this one was frightening. The head meat cutter indicated to me that he had been having difficulty with gross profit but that he was resolving the problem. I later found out how. I was grinding beef through a coarse grind into a very large hopper, with the meat going into large aluminum tubs underneath the grinding head. After the coarse grind, the head must be pulled off the grinder, the cutting blade and coarse plate are taken off, and a new cutting blade and a fine grinding plate are put on. Before I could turn the grinder on again to finish up the grind, the head meat cutter interrupted me. "Wait a minute; I have to doctor it up a bit. I have some stuff here that I put in it. It kind of keeps it from turning dark." So he pulled out a dirty mop bucket with a ladle in it and proceeded to dump a white compound from a box into about 2 gallons of water, mixing it up with a broom handle. He lifted the bucket off the floor and threw it into the ground beef tub and began to mix and churn the ground beef with his hands so he could spread the solution evenly through the grind.

I asked him, "What the hell are you doing?"

He replied, "This stuff acts as a preservative. I can leave that ground beef out there two weeks and it will still be bright."

I asked him what it was and he said it was industrial floor cleaner, the same type of cleaner they use to clean the bubble gum, residue, and dirt from the hard surface of a floor. This whole episode seemed like something from *Twilight Zone*. I couldn't believe it was happening, but the sick truth was—it was happening.

The only time people obey the law is when they have good inspections and regulations, or if they feel they can quit that job and chance starving for a little while. I have gotten myself in trouble trying to improve safety and sanitation. It was getting to a point where I was weary. I just went along with the system. I am sure many people who work in restaurants and other food industries feel this way when they find out that "Consumer Fair Practices" is just a nice group of words. I have often wondered why the Health Department doesn't regularly check the various "fresh" meat items to find out if they have harmful additives in them. But maybe these conditions will change someday. The head meat cutter mentioned that no one had ever complained to him about the meat. But then again, maybe bad meat takes months to affect the metabolism of the body.

Senate Bill 77, passed by the Seventy-Fourth General Assembly of the State of Missouri, defines "adulterated" as being any meat or meat products which "is made impure by an admixture of a foreign substance which renders it injurious to health."[14]

Consumer Reports in 1971 stated that a shockingly large percentage of hamburger it purchased for testing was well on the way to putrefaction. A good number of the samples contained more fat than unadulterated hamburger would normally; in fact, some samples contained more fat than the law allowed. The report hinted that at least some ground meat labeled as chuck may have been something else.[15]

According to the Federal Register, a product is adulterated if:

> any valuable constituent has been in whole or in part omitted or abstracted therefrom, or any substance has been substituted, wholly or in part therefor, or damage or inferiority has been concealed in any manner, or any substance has been added thereto or mixed or packed therewith so as to increase its bulk or weight or reduce its quality or strength or make it appear better or of greater value than it is.[16]

The Federal Register indicates that products will not be misbranded and this includes false or misleading labeling.

The states have adopted similar wording in their meat and poultry inspection programs, but the adulterations are still taking place daily in retail supermarkets.

Inspection has improved in the wholesale packing houses over the years. Unfortunately, the same cannot be said of inspection of supermarkets. Supermarket inspections are spotty and sometimes nonexistent.

CHAPTER V

"THE HOG"

I looked forward to the summer of 1965 because I would be able to save money for college by working vacation relief for the second national chain again. I would work in one store for a week or two and then move on to another, covering for the full-time men who were on vacation.

The first store I worked in during the summer of 1965, like most stores, had a tendency to end up with a lot of dark meat from reworks pulled from the meat case. "Reworks" are dark meat, outdated, lacking freshness or otherwise unsuited for sale to the general public. Most companies sold their dark meat to local restaurants or special customers, sometimes called "honey customers." This practice would help the company's gross profit and the restaurant's gross profit as well. The restaurants would buy such meat for less than half of what they would pay if they bought good meat from a packing house or from a restaurant supplier.

This practice is illegal. In many of these cases, the meat sold to restaurants is putrid and it is usually transported in an unrefrigerated station wagon or truck. The meat sold has lost its case life, it is outdated, and in many cases it is not fit for human consumption.

It gets very hot in Missouri and in Kansas in the summer. The temperature in a station wagon on a 100-degree day must be staggering. The procedure is nearly always the same; the people from the restaurant come to the back door and ring the meat bell. The head meat cutter is summoned to the back door, and together they discuss the weather and baseball and sometimes exchange a couple of jokes. They walk back to a large walk-in freezer and pull out boxes of frozen dark and rotten meat. They weigh the meat on a platform scale and figure out the price. The restaurant owner goes to the front of the store with a piece of paper which has a price. The meat is paid for and the receipt is brought back to the meat department before the station wagon or car can be loaded. Everyone is happy. This sight was nothing new, for I had seen it over and over again in almost every store.

That same summer I worked in the company's largest store. We had been saving dark meat that was unacceptable for sale to the customers. The cutters complained each time they had to save a piece of bad meat, because they knew where it was going. One day I threw some rotten pork spare ribs in a bone barrel; they were so covered with slime that I couldn't hold onto my knife after touching them, and it just slipped out of my hand and fell on the floor. The head meat cutter said, "Don't throw them away; I have a home for them."

A meat cutter who had witnessed this incident told me I'd have to be more careful if I wanted to be sure of throwing bad meat away. He said, "Next time, bury them with some fat and bones. Since we found this new place, we don't throw *anything* away. This lady that buys all the meat is a real lowlife bitch—white trash, if you know what I mean." The men were forced to sell

82 / Meat Eaters are Threatened

the rotten meat, so it seems they were taking out their frustrations on the lady who was buying the meat. But why? I couldn't figure it out.

When she called to say she would be in the next day to pick up the meat, she asked if we had any bad chickens. Since we didn't, she had to buy two boxes of fresh chickens. The guys were joking about that the rest of the day, saying, "I hope it doesn't break the old bitch."

The next day came and I was curious about the old lady. As soon as she arrived, the men started calling her all kinds of names, but she was on the other side of the partition and couldn't hear them. I was still in the dark, but I knew I would get a few clues if I would be patient.

The first clue was: "I'd sooner die than send my mother to a place like that." It is hard to hear everything in a meat market because of all the machines, so when they are shut off, you listen twice as hard. The next comment was a cincher: "The state ought to watch these old folks' homes a lot closer."

I couldn't believe what I had heard. I walked around the meat block and asked the men if that was where all the rotten pork and dark meat was going, and they said, "That's right; the old bitch buys the stuff like it is going out of style".

From that point on, I began to get nosy about everything. I hadn't forgotten those spareribs I had tried to throw away. The bad thing about rotten pork is that it can kill you even if it is cooked.

About a month later I was working in a store where I witnessed another common practice. The meat bell rang and the head meat cutter said, "Jon, catch the back door. That's the supervisor with some chucks for us." I opened the meat door, and there was the meat supervisor standing next to this beat-up old green car. The trunk was open and flies were swarming all around the meat. The meat was difficult to lift out of the trunk of the car, partly because each beef chuck was a large packer chuck weighing between 95 and 125 pounds. But the main reason the meat was difficult to lift was because the temperature that day was in the 90s and God only knows how long the meat had been left in the trunk. It was like an oven—except ovens aren't rusted out and full of bacteria, flies, and dirt. I tried to scrape some of the flies and dirt off the meat with a meat scraper, but the supervisor said, "I'm not paying you to mess around. We have customers to take care of."

As I have mentioned earlier, it is against the law to ship fresh meat intended for human consumption in unrefrigerated vehicles. Yet this is a common occurrence in the stores I have worked in.

The summer was drawing to a close, but before it was over, I had the opportunity to work for one of the men I heard talked about most. It seemed that nobody ever said anything good about him, but he did have a good gross profit. They called him "The Hog." I soon found out why. He was cheating the packing companies, the customers, and his own company. The man would sell dark beef to the sausage company delivery man, who sold the old ground beef to a restaurant. One day we were grinding beef and he threw about 30 pounds of frozen beef kidneys in with the grind. He went back into the cooler and brought out a tray of dark meat and mixed it all up with bulk fat and frozen shank meat. When it was all ground together, it looked like a normal grind of ground beef. The Hog lifted his head from the grinder and said, "I'm going for 26 percent this time." He was talking about his gross profit. I started cutting chucks and The Hog walked over to the power saw and cut two neck roasts. Half of each roast was bone.

The next week we found we were stuck with about a hundred rotten chickens. I suggested we send them back and get credit, but he said we needed them in the case. They smelled just like rotten eggs; the air was thick with the odor. He said, "When I get through with these, you won't know they're bad." He filled up the sink with cold water, dumped three boxes of chickens in, and covered them with baking soda. He mixed the baking soda around and around. When he was finished, he said, "This kind of brings them back to life." He pulled the plug out, drained the water off, bagged them—and sold them.

He was great fun to watch when the beef order came in. He would never let anyone else check the beef order. This seemed odd, for he was a fat man and it was hard work. Coffee-break time came, and this provided an excuse to watch the old pro. This guy couldn't help coming up with a good "G.P." (gross profit); he knew every trick. While the truck driver wasn't looking, The Hog would cut off "cod fat" from under the flank of the hindquarters. When he set his tare weight to subtract the weight of the steel hooks, the driver would watch, but he never figured out why the weight was short. He would write a report on the shortage, and The Hog would get credit. When the orders came in over weight, The Hog would slip the driver a couple of dark steaks and all was forgotten.

The store was in a predominantly black neighborhood. The head meat cutter seemed to get away with many things that would get him into trouble in another part of the city. Part of the reason for a high gross profit for stores in black neighborhoods is that the classified base for gross profit is higher. These stores sell more items that carry a higher profit margin. Black neighborhoods buy large quantities of pork, including neck bones, spare ribs, pigs' feet, pigs' ears, pork chops, butts, and hocks. All of these are high-profit items.

These items were checked one Monday morning and

most of the pork rewraps were putrid, but The Hog was notorious for pushing off bad meat on customers.

If you had walked into the cooler, you couldn't have helped noticing a carcass of lamb lying in the chicken drain. Looking around, you could have seen dark stew meat and cube steak material lying on pans without any oxygenic paper placed between the meat to help stop it from turning dark.

The Hog wanted a pork sausage grind next. The sausage was seasoned with too much seasoning, but I could see why—the pork was slimy. I started to dump the rotten pork trimmings in the bone barrel because I was fed up, but he said, "Do you want to get me busted because of bad gross? Put these two pans of pork fat with the trim. Sausage isn't any good unless it has some fat in it." Sausage fat content according to the *Federal Register*, is defined:

> Fresh pork sausage, prepared with fresh pork or frozen pork, or both, not including pork by-products, and may be seasoned with condimental substances as permitted under Part 318 of this subchapter [of the *Federal Register*]. It shall not be made with any lot of product which, in the aggregate, contains more than 50% trimmable fat, that is fat which can be removed by thorough, practicable trimming and sorting.[1]

Even though the maximum fat content permitted by the government is 50 percent, I personally feel that the figure is far too high and that 40 percent is a more reasonable and acceptable figure.

Hams Ain't What They Used to Be

The last thing I remember that summer of 1965 was a ham sale that didn't quite make it.

Hams have changed a lot over the years. I have personally made homemade cured and smoked hams by the old methods. The commercial techniques of ham processing used today have lost both the taste and the quality produced by these older methods. Years ago ham was cured in salts, sugars, and spices with the natural juices of the product forming a brine or pickle. Another process included soaking the ham in a brine solution for a few months and then, after curing and smoking it for flavor, drying it to prevent spoilage.

But about forty years ago a new concept for hams was developed. It involved pumping curing solution into the ham with needles inserted into the tissues. A newer method developed out of the old idea, and a needle was inserted directly into the main artery. This new concept allowed the large and small processors an opportunity to cheat the consumer. By 1937 overpumping of hams was becoming a major problem. Finally, in July 1950, the Department of Agriculture established a new regulation requiring that pumped hams be reduced to their original weight, or "green weight," as it is referred to in the trade.[2]

But in 1950 another new idea became popular. Phosphates were added to the brine so the tissues would absorb more water. The phosphates also made it very difficult for the consumer to determine whether the ham had been adulterated.

Later, because of public outcry, Secretary of Agriculture Orville L. Freeman, called a public hearing. Some called pumping hams full of water "governmental approval of cheating." Senator Maurine Neuberger pointed out that in Portland 12,000 pounds of water could be purchased for 35 cents; however, 35 cents is the price of merely the water contained in a 5-pound ham costing 79 cents a pound. She argued that ham sales probably totaled $875 million (in 1960) and that

10 percent of that figure would be $87.5 million worth of federally inspected water.[3]

The order was rescinded by Secretary Freeman, but Armour & Co. took the case to court and beat the federal government.[4] Today hams may contain up to 10 percent water without being labeled "Imitation." All federally inspected hams containing water must have "Ham—water added" placed on them.

In the meat markets I have worked in over the last ten years, I have seen very few hams with "Ham—water added" on them. Many hams today are processed in intrastate plants, which are beyond federal control. Many of these hams contain three to four times the maximum allowable water content according to federal requirements. This is profit for the packer—but the consumer is being cheated and nothing is being done to stop this adulteration.

The supermarkets' adulteration of the same hams make the packing companies look like good guys. This practice has taken place in *every* store I've worked in during the past ten years, and it must be stopped.

The Hog had three grocery cartfuls of hams left from a ham sale a month before. They had been wrapped and rewrapped a dozen times, but we couldn't sell them. By this time the hams were slick with bacteria and green and white mold. Many of the hams had dark spots on them from where the mold had eaten into the tissues.

I was ordered to fill a large sink up with water and to scrub the hams with a scrub brush until I removed all the mold. Some of the mold came off, but the black spots remained. The hams were putrid, and the pleasant smoke flavor had been dissipated by decomposition and adulteration. The hams were so full of contaminated water that when you squeezed them on the face side, they resembled a sponge full of water. The "boss" brought back three bottles of "liquid smoke" from the grocery shelf and ordered me to doctor them up and rub the smoke all over the surface of the hams.

The hams were rotten and there was no way anyone could argue the fact. However, for weeks after that we sold those hams. Finally, when we couldn't sell any more, we sliced some of them and diced some others for ham seasoning. And then he called a local restaurant to take the balance off his hands. There were 20 hams left—all were sold to a restaurant.

Such practices take place daily in retail supermarkets in this country, and as in the adulteration of the sausage, gross profit is the motive.

The pork sausage being made in retail supermarkets is not produced under the watchful eye of either state or federal inspection; in fact, many stores go from six months to a year without any inspection at all. I question the credibility of local health department inspections. The markets they inspect pay large sums of taxes to the local governments. For supermarket inspections to be totally objective, they should come from a higher governmental source which cannot be hurt by the closing of local establishments. If there were good inspections, the practices would not continue.

These and countless numbers of other incidents of adulteration take place daily in every state in this country.

The state of Missouri can't be held totally responsible for a company's being remiss in the preparation and handling of fresh meat products. The major portion of responsibility should be upon the companies—they have an obligation in the public interest to police their district supervisors and managers to stop these adulterations.

If the companies claim that customers will have to pay more money for meat if the adulteration of meat stops, then these companies should visit a number of the better USDA-inspected wholesale processing plants to see how meat should be processed.

Chapter VI

THE REAL JUNGLE

In 1966 I was scheduled to work for a large new store in Kansas.

The store was new, all right; it hadn't been opened for more than two months. Everywhere you looked there was new equipment—two new power saws, a computerized scaling machine, an automatic wrapper, a large, stainless steel ground beef grinder and a shiny new cube steak machine. It was just like Christmas all over again. I was introduced to the crew and production started. I was working on cube steaks, a rather simple task; you merely drop thin beef fillets into the machine and retract your fingers and catch them at the bottom—the steak, that is, not the fingers.

I found myself running out of cube material, so I made an about-face toward the cooler to pick up some more, but before I could take a step, my feet slid apart and I fell to my knees. The floor was coated with cod fat and suet. I asked why they hadn't cleaned the floor. The answer was, "Ever since grand opening there just hasn't been enough time."

Later on in the day, the girl who was wrapping fell and landed flat on her back behind the wrapping machine. She took a long time to get up. She complained that her back hurt her all day, and she missed several weeks of work.

That night the head meat cutter had a detailed cutting list long enough to keep three good men busy. I finished most of the cutting list, but I deviated from the clean-up orders. They were, "Rake the sawdust if you have time and wipe off the saws and put the guts of the saws in a grocery cart and wheel them into the beef cooler. Do the same with the ground beef grinder." The union stated in the contract that an ample amount of time should be given to clean-up. I thought I would find out what "ample amount of time" meant. First I swept the entire floor to remove the loose sawdust. I then took meat block scrapers and scraped for one hour on my hands and knees to remove the cod fat and suet. I used a shovel to pick it up; it filled two chicken boxes with fat. I wanted to see for myself just how much fat had been imbedded into the floor, so I weighed the boxes. The total of both boxes came to 47 pounds. I deviated further from the head meat cutter's orders by cleaning all the equipment. This, too, took a lot of hard work, not to mention cleaning solution, hot water, and scrub brushes. The last thing I did was wash the floor. It was all I could do just to crawl out to the car, my back hurt so much from all that scraping and scrubbing.

The next day all hell broke loose. The head meat cutter said, "I could fire you for what you did last night. To hell with clean-up, you just cut the goddamn meat. If I'd wanted it cleaned up, it would have been on the list."

It was a big joke around the district that I had cleaned up the market and scrubbed the floor. The unfortunate part of this story is that this man is now a meat buyer for one of the three largest food retailers in the country.

They May Be Number Three—But Watch Out!

After finishing two weeks vacation relief in that store, I moved on to bigger and better things. The next Kansas store was one of the company's most dilapidated stores. It was in a poor neighborhood. The cutting room had no refrigeration. The knives would get so slick from the warm fat that they would jump out of your hand like a bar of soap.

This was certainly a safety hazard, but the real problem wasn't safety—it was health and sanitation. Old Joe (the relief head meat cutter) and I would try to clean all the equipment, but because of time, it was difficult to do a good job. Every morning when we came back into the market, there would be a few little friends waiting in the saw, the grinder, the meat slicer, and sometimes even in the meat block. I'm referring to fly eggs, better known as maggots. It's not a very pleasant sight, but what can you do when the temperature of the cutting area in an old store like that one reaches 80 to 85 degrees? But don't relax and assume that the problem is limited to old stores. I have worked in a number of large, new independent food chain stores that use this open cutting area approach, and the same problem exists there, even though they have cooling coils and blowers. The temperature is not lowered sufficiently to kill the flies and other pests. These open cutting practices are outmoded and ineffectual. The companies who have adopted open cutting should reappraise their philosophy, because health and sanitary conditions cannot be maintained without sufficient refrigeration. The open cutting philosophy evidently was initiated as a gimmick to allow customers the feeling of involvement or observation of the meat cutting operation. This is a false front. You see only what they want you to see. The company could keep this concept and protect the public better if they enclosed the area with glass.

The Little Meat Processor

The year 1967 was important to me because I was starting work on my master's degree. My only problem was that I was spending more money than I earned cutting meat in Kansas City on weekends and summers. I couldn't keep up with the cost of college, so I took a job at a small, family-owned processing plant in a small town in Missouri. The plant sold both retail and wholesale. I was hired as a journeyman meat cutter, and I worked each afternoon after classes.

One day I had arrived for work early, so I went into the kill floor. The boss was butchering a steer. Meat cutters don't generally slaughter; by the time the meat cutter gets the animal, it is usually well bled and chilled, making it easier to cut. This was the second time I had watched a slaughter. The one time before had been on a tour through a large Kansas City packing house.

This was also the first time I had been so close, and I found it frightening to watch. The cattle were brought into a maze of wooden shoots by prodding them with long sticks. When the animal reached a certain point, a gate was closed behind it, separating it from the herd. The animal was prodded until it reached a drop platform; then the boss shot it in the head, usually between the eyes. The animals would thrust around even after being shot several times. Then the drop platform separated in the middle and the animal fell to the kill floor below. Here the work crew would tie chains around the animal's feet and spread-eagle it so they could start skinning. The animal was slashed through the neck and hung with the head down. This step is called bleeding. After bleeding, they would bring in a large 55-gallon barrel, place it under the animal, and sever the animal's mid-section so all the innards would fall into the barrel. the hoofs and the head were cut off; then the animal was split down the center of the back into two sides which were pushed into a large cooler to chill before further processing.

Many small, family-owned and -operated processing plants across the country are not inspected regularly by the states. This small plant was never inspected by any city or state inspection group. Federal inspection involves only plants that ship across state boundaries, so federal inspectors also had never inspected the plant.

The inside of the plant was not refrigerated; only the large holding cooler had refrigeration. The cutting room area where I worked was very hot, about 85 to 95 degrees until the sun went down. It was impossible to fight bacteria growth in those temperatures. Flies, cockroaches, and large black water bugs were always crawling through the ground beef tubs which were placed next to my cutting block. The cooler had large tubfuls of kidneys and livers. In the corner there was a broken, rusty drum full of water, blood, and beef livers. The beef hung in straight lines from front to back of the cooler. Before I could break the beef into four quarters and hindquarter sections, it had to be pushed out to the cutting room. It took two people to push the heavy beef. When the beef reached the cutting room, it would drag along the floor; and because of the lack of power equipment and proper hoist, much of the beef fell on the floor when it was being separated into quarter sections.

We were selling hamburger patties to two national drive-in restaurants in town. A large percentage of good beef portions went into the hamburger, including pieces which, in a supermarket, normally would go into cube steaks and beef stew meat. The only reason the boss put these pieces in was that he couldn't sell so much stew meat and cube steaks, so it would be wasted if he didn't put it into hamburger. That was the only good thing about the hamburger processed there.

He would put melts and head meat in the grind on occasions, and if someone found an abscessed beef or pork liver, it was never thrown away. Beef cheeks were also put in the hamburger. After the meat was ground, he dumped large amounts of cereal and meal into it and added water; and then he ran it through the large grinder.

After the fine grind, the meat was put into a hopper of an automatic pattying machine, and then the patties were placed in a box to be picked up later by the restaurant. Because of the flies and other pests found constantly in the beef trimmings, there must have been disease-causing organisms in each restaurant order.

What Did You Say Your Animal Died Of?

Whenever a farmer had a diseased or dying animal, we would get a call and the boss would take it off the farmer's hands for $50 to $100.

It was sickening and illegal, but there was no inspection of the plant, so it continued for one year and probably would still be going on if the family hadn't moved away and sold the business.

Similar conditions exist throughout the country; and even with the present inspection system, things are looking pretty unhealthy for the consumer.

The April 20, 1963, issue of *The National Provisioner* described conditions which plague New York and other states. Dr. William E. Jennings (director of the New York Division of Meat Inspection) remarked in the article that some conditions observed in New York make *The Jungle* look mild; that while the legislators were slashing the budget request, dead animals were being skinned out a block from the Capitol and sold for hamburger. Out of 30 random samples of hamburger picked up in one week, 26 were found to be "embalmed" with sulphite. Also detected were frankfurters containing about 20 percent skin, additive-loaded hams retaining five to ten times the amount of water permitted; sausage with up to 20 percent cereal, and products containing hog blood, lungs, niacin, water, detergent, antibiotics, and so on.

Dr. Jennings added that chemical-wise, you name it and New York has it. He estimated that about 90 percent of the uninspected processed meat sold in the states bears deceptive labeling.[1]

About 85 percent of the meat animals slaughtered in the United States are slaughtered under federal inspection, and approximately 75 percent of meat processed is also subject to inspection.

While I was busy observing meat being adulterated in Missouri, Betty Furness, the President's Assistant for Consumer Affairs, was testifying before the Senate for stronger meat inspection for the public. "I contend that the American consumer who has discovered that Federal law does not cover all meat is shocked to learn of the results. He is shocked to read about the filthy conditions in some slaughter and processing plants, about the sick and diseased cattle which can become meat on American tables, (and) about the potential danger this holds for American health."[2]

The small Missouri plant I worked in was not alone in its deceptive processing operation. Ralph Nader alleges that a meat processor in Illinois that same year, 1967, was actually specializing in "last resort" purchasing of "4-D" animals (dead, diseased, dying or disabled).

Excerpts from the 1967 surveys are illustrative: A state of Illinois meat inspection program has been operating for several years and includes inspection of slaughtering and processing operations. The city of Chicago's Board of Health has also conducted a meat inspection program. The Chicago authorities do not consider the state program acceptable and do not permit the sale of state-inspected products within the city of Chicago unless the products are accepted by Chicago inspectors. The lack of recognition creates political sensitivity—and problems. For example, Chicago authorities were quick to tone down and minimize the discovery that (blank) in (blank) had used boneless beef covered with powdered charcoal as sausage raw material . . . (blank) of (blank), Illinois, is known to specialize in the slaughter of down and disabled animals. (Blank) is well acquainted within the community of 4-D dealers; the (blank) of (Blank), Illinois operates under state inspection and specializes in the slaughter of 4-D swine.

Nader was asked, why don't state legislators appropriate even barely adequate funds? His answer: Largely because segments of the meat industry have no interest in adequate meat inspection.[3] Bad meat is just too good for business.

Dr. Stanford Mesrill of the Maine Department of Agriculture stated:

> We're not giving the consumer enough protection. But if the industry were to support us, we would have a new law tomorrow. Too many state departments of agriculture have been afflicted with the corrosive effect of political patronage degrading the professional quality of personnel. The mantle of states' rights too often is worn as a cloak for patronage incompetence and industry-indentured policies.[4]

We've Come a Long Way Over the Years—Haven't We?

Some very disgusting conditions have been disclosed over the past few years. The following incidents, reported in the *Packing House Worker*, were used in testimony before a subcommittee of the Senate Committee on Agriculture and Forestry in 1967.

Washington, April 1966—Two men who pleaded guilty to charges of transporting tainted meat from dead and diseased animals across statelines were fired and given suspended sentences for violating the Federal Meat Inspection Act. The U. S. Department of Agriculture's Consumer and Marketing Service alleged that the two men shipped 4,400 pounds of boneless meat that had not been federally inspected from Greely, Washington, to Cheyenne, Wyoming. It was intended for human consumption.

If the men had confined their activities within the borders of one state, they might still be running a profitable business from adulterated meat. The Meat Inspection Act provides only that all meat crossing a state boundary must be federally inspected. The law does not stipulate that meat slaughtered and consumed within statelines must be inspected for wholesomeness and purity.

Pennsylvania, May 1966—Seven men were accused of repacking more than 10 million pounds of horse meat shipped in from Mexico and of selling it to processors as boneless beef, from 1962 to 1964. They were indicted by a grand jury. The meat was sold as boneless beef to processors in Ohio, Pennsylvania, and Maryland. The profit made on the meat was estimated at $1 million, netting 10 to 12 cents a pound.

Six of the men were indicted on 23 counts charging them with conspiracy, fraud by wire, and violations of the Horse Meat Act and the Meat Inspection Act. The seventh man was charged with a 14-count indictment.

Boneless beef and boneless horse meat cannot be distinguished from each other without chemical analysis in a laboratory.

Washington, D.C., March 1967—A North Carolina meat packer was found guilty on three counts of violation of the Federal Meat Inspection Act.

The man was fined $3,000, and officials said he had "consistently shipped uninspected barbecued pork products from Louisburg [North Carolina] to South Hill, Virginia."[5]

98 / Meat Eaters are Threatened

Some surveys in 1962 and 1967 by the U. S. Department of Agriculture revealed alarming facts about poor conditions in the meat industry. Here are findings of some mandatory inspections which were reported by Ralph Nader before a Senate subcommittee.

Virginia (At a large national producer)—The report stated, in part, that the meat grinder bearings had much encrusted putrid material which would easily result in bacterial contamination of the ground meat. Sausage was hung on unclean aluminum smoke sticks, and no attempt whatsoever was made to clean the sausage mixer.

Some beef cuts hanging in the cooler showed evidence of soilage while in transit and had not been reconditioned by removing the soiled portions. Other unsanitary conditions noted were ceilings with leaks and dripping on exposed meat, causing serious contamination. Some cockroaches were observed in the curing cellar where exposed meat is handled and stored.

Florida—The tank room had maggots present on the floor, in barrels (condemned), in the screw conveyor, and in the "pre-breaker". Flies were present everywhere. There was also dirty beef present from improper trimming and washing on the killing floor. Rust and grease on trolly hooks had been transferred to hocks, rounds and ribs of carcasses.

Texas—On the killing floor, the hands of the hog brisket splitter and hog headers were covered with blood and hair due to infrequent washing of hands. Carcasses and tubs of meat were seen to be contaminated with drippings from the ceiling. Paint, scale, rust, and plaster were falling down from the walls and ceiling on the product. At least 50 hogs were split and deheaded with no attempt made on the part of the house employees to clean their hands and knives from the contamination of blood and hair.

The offal was found to be grossly contaminated with

fecal material, metal, filings, hair, hide, dirt, and so forth.

The state inspector felt that all of the offal should have been condemned. However, he took no action.

In the ham processing department, the inspector had no way of determining whether or not hams came back to "green weight" after pumping and smoking. The condemned product was not tanked under supervision.

The plant was operating beyond capacity. In all departments, products were stacked on tables so high that at times they fell on the floor.[6]

These poor conditions exist throughout the United States in both large and small processing plants. Ralph Nader made the important point in his testimony before the Senate subcommittee when he said:

> When considering the public health, it is very dangerous to wait until there are direct connections, which often can never be made. Years ago in our cities and in our states and in Europe, we cleaned up the filth, before we knew what the connection was to typhoid and other epidemic diseases.... As a matter of fact, it is almost a routine paragraph in many newspapers, at least once a week, of mass cases of food poisoning, where people are not seriously stricken but they are certainly discomforted and may spend one or two days in the hospital. That happens very frequently.
>
> I think there is certainly enough evidence of people becoming sick, both in terms of localized epidemics and in terms of individual afflictions.[7]

Nader had received a letter from a girl who purchased some pork at a local supermarket near Columbia University, and she indicated that she had come down with trichinosis. She had written, "It was not a slum area. It was in a very reputable residential area."

Mr. Nader went on:

> I think there is enough evidence to show the need for strong immediate legislation now.... I often wonder why states are willing to take so many chances when public health is at stake. I do not think that the states would ever give the federal government 60 years to clean up the meat situation if the roles were reversed, and I think the federal government now should, certainly, have every reason and constitutional authority to take over the meat inspection of plants in this country and then say to the states, "If you really show capability and willingness, then you can pull it away from us, in terms of intrastate products."

Mr. Nader was asked by Senator Byrd, "At this point in your judgment, how many states have adequate meat inspection laws?"

Mr. Nader stated, "My judgment coincides with that of the Department of Agriculture, which does not think that any state has an adequate inspection law, even California."[8]

Partly because of the poor conditions described in testimony on meat inspection before the Senate we have a new law, the Federal Meat Inspection Act. Amended by Congress in December 1967 with the subsequent passage of the Wholesome Meat Act, this law will for the most part stop or hinder state-inspected meat from passing interstate or even into federally inspected establishments within the same state.

Under the new law, states must develop a program "at least equal to federal inspection programs" for their intrastate plants within two years after the laws are enacted. According to this, the states were to comply by

December 15, 1969. If the states showed significant attempts toward reaching the goal they were given an extension of one year, until December 15, 1970. Only 3 states made the first deadline. Of the others, 46 states were granted an additional year to comply. If the states did not comply, the federal government was to take over inspection. In the case of Pennsylvania, the federal government took over inspection on July 17, 1972.[9]

The present Federal Meat Inspection Act provides a federal-state cooperative venture, with the federal government giving the states technical assistance and financial aid up to 50 percent of the total cost of the inspection program. The states would not have to put up the money if they would not mind government takeover.

This new meat inspection act will help stop or decrease some of the conditions being perpetrated against the public by the intrastate wholesale packing house industry, but that is little consolation, because the American public rarely buys directly from a processing plant.

The public buys from the retail supermarkets, who take this meticulous USDA- or state-inspected meat and do whatever they please with the meat products.

Unless strict inspection is brought down through all levels of meat processing, especially to retail supermarkets, which are the last link before human consumption, previous inspection is of no use.

Chapter VII

WHOLESALE VERSUS RETAIL

The customers see only what a company wants them to see. The modern retail supermarket meat department presents a unique façade that hasn't really changed in over fifty years, with the exception of a little more glass and stainless steel out front to impress the customers. There has been change in processing, but much of the change is for the benefit of profit, sacrificing product quality.

Chickens, for example, used to be cut by hand, jointing them with a knife. Today, chickens are cut on a high-speed power saw, which rips through the bones and tissues, leaving small pieces of bone throughout the meat. Why did the companies change? Because it costs too much money to cut by hand. That may be true, if you feel that a 2-second difference is a significant matter. How much money could 2 seconds in labor cost the companies or the public if the cost were passed on to the customer? Not much more than a penny per chicken.

Then again, the breast bone used to be removed routinely from cut-up chickens. Today, you pay extra in most retail markets if the breast bone is removed.

In 1961, the meat cutters in most stores skinned the beef liver and separated the tough connecting tissue. Today most retail supermarkets don't take the time to skin or clean the liver. Many stores don't even cut the liver with a knife any more; they just freeze it and cut it on a high-speed saw. This increases the companies' profit by saving on labor and by selling the entire liver—the customer buys the waste.

Most rolled roasts were tied with string by hand, so when you cooked and cut the roast, it didn't fall apart. No such luck today—many of the supermarkets now use a loose netting. It saves them a few pennies in labor, they contend.

Cube steaks used to be always seamed out, with the tough sinew tissue removed, because regardless of how many times it would be run through the cubing machine, the sinew could not be chewed when the steak was eaten. Today when you eat a cube steak, you find the sinew. It feels like little nylon cords.

Remember how little fat and bone there was on almost all cuts of meat about ten years ago? Today the word in most retail supermarkets is, "Don't chime the bone" and "Heavy on the trim." Perhaps these are conditions we will have to live with. On the other hand, there are many fine things being done in the wholesale industry which aren't taking place in the retail end of the business.

The average customer knows very little about meat, although he does think the business has come a long way over the past half century, especially since *The Jungle*, by Upton Sinclair. *The Jungle* was instrumental in bringing some change to the packing house industry. The first meat inspection act was passed on March 18, 1907, primarily because of Sinclair's exposure of poor conditions in the industry.[1]

If you were to visit an average packing house today, you would find men working in white smocks, with knives in their hands—like their counterparts in the retail meat markets. But this would be the only similarity between the wholesale and retail ends of the business.

Unlike retail meat markets, the wholesale cutting rooms are much cooler in temperature. In five wholesale plants in central Connecticut, the temperatures were in the range of about 35 to 48 degrees in the cutting rooms. Temperatures in the retail supermarkets fall in the range of about 42 to 68 degrees in the enclosed cutting areas, while temperatures as high as 80 degrees are found in a number of open cutting-area rooms in many new supermarkets and in a great many small local markets.

A wholesale plant in the great majority of cases is susceptible to more inspections in one week than the average supermarket receives in a year. This keeps the industry on its toes.

104 / Meat Eaters are Threatened

If you were to walk into a wholesale plant, you would notice that their floors are much cleaner than floors in the retail meat departments. There is no sawdust on the floors to breed bacteria. All the men wear some kind of hat to keep hair out of the meat. The meat cutters are standing on rust-proof metal grids. All the equipment is cleaned immediately after use. In a wholesale plant I visited, I observed pattying machines and ground beef grinders being cleaned following use. All boxes were placed on rust-proof steel racks, most of which were galvanized metal or aluminum. The meat blocks were all composed of a nonporous substance which is less likely to harbor bacteria than wood is. The blocks were housed in galvanized and stainless steel frames. The frames and the tops were separated and cleaned each night.

In this wholesale plant, all equipment was cleaned each day with a special nontoxic cleaner and hot water. Many supermarkets find it easier, and perhaps cheaper, to use Mr. Clean, Top Job, Lestoil and ammonia to clean their meat blocks and equipment. I have been directed to use these products in about 50 stores over the past ten years, because the companies wouldn't purchase a safe, nontoxic cleaner. While these products may be excellent for cleaning almost anything from dirty whitewall tires to hard-to-remove stains, they should not come in contact with the prepared meat meant for human consumption.

Employees working for the large chain I worked for use these harsh detergents to clean their equipment, including power saws, meat blocks, ground beef grinders, and cubing machines. The detergent solutions are not rinsed off with clear water. They are wiped off with a block scraper, towel, or apron, thus exposing the meat out on the meat blocks and other equipment to harsh contamination. For the protection of the public health, all handlers or processors of meat products must stop using these detergents to clean processing equipment.

In a wholesale plant, all the floors in the cutting areas and large coolers are swept and cleaned with hot water and nontoxic cleaning solution each night. The walls are covered with porcelain, stainless steel, or some other rust-proof substance. Most plants are going to stainless steel today because it is very easy to clean and it holds up well. In the retail supermarkets the walls, and especially the floors, are rarely ever cleaned in the meat department. This seems odd, because most supermarkets clean and wax the customer area floors each week. But perhaps this is because the customers only see that part of the store area floor.

I lifted the meat blocks from their frame at the National Packing Company plant on Main Street in Hartford, Connecticut, and noticed no detectable odor or appearance of the men's being negligent in their cleanup. The floor, walls and all equipment were exceptionally clean.[2]

Poultry is never stored with beef, pork, or veal in a processing plant. This is not the case in retail meat departments. Beef is never cut on the same saw used for pork in the wholesale plants. Pork and beef are cut on the same saws in retail supermarkets; in fact, many retail markets have only one power saw. All meat items including pork, beef, veal, lamb, poultry, and fish are cut on the power saws interchangeably. This is a good way to exchange bacteria contamination from one meat source to another. Trichina worms could possibly be spread from pork to other meat items in this manner.

The beef coolers of the wholesale packers are very neat and clean, and provide more access space than do those in retail meat departments. All the beef cuts are arranged in order with hindquarters in one section, forequarters in another; with chucks, rounds, loins, plates, ribs, and flanks similarly organized and separated. While each plant I have visited had a different beef hanging arrangement, all seemed well organized. The cooler walls in all the wholesale packing plants were immaculate.

The following is an account of an unwarned inspection I carried out at a USDA-inspected wholesale packer on August 27, 1971, between the hours of 10 a.m. and 4 p.m. I would like to thank Mr. Joseph Negro, general manager of Home Pride Provisions Company, Stafford Springs, Connecticut, for the excellent job his company and its personnel are doing in their concern for proper care and handling of all levels of their operation.

No one knew me at the plant, so I introduced myself, explaining that I had been a retail meat cutter for the past ten years and that I would like to see how the meat is handled before stores received shipment. I was given full access to the establishment for six hours.

This plant, unlike the National Packing Company, which I had visited on June 23, 1971, was classified as a total processor. They had a USDA federal inspector there during all slaughter operations. This man was a veterinarian, and each animal was inspected with great care before and after slaughter. Other plants I visited were also exceptionally clean, primarily because of the increasing concern over the years over winning the faith of the public.

The state inspection on the wholesale level in Connecticut and in many other states has been brought up to a higher level of excellence because of the amendment of the Wholesome Meat Inspection Act originally passed in 1907. As explained in Chapter VI, the 1967 Wholesome Meat Inspection law made states bring their standards up to the federal level. While this has caused some smaller operations in a number of states to go out of the meat business entirely, it has been beneficial for the people in this country, who could otherwise purchase meat from any source, large or small, with no controls over whether it had been adulterated in any one of a thousand ways. Those people who would like to dilute the new law, who are "concerned" for the small operator's plight for their own reasons, should be a little more aware of the dangers involved in an unhealthily run establishment.

All of the plants I had visited, and all meat processing plants in the state of Connecticut, are subject to state inspection. The state inspectors in the intrastate plants (shipping within state lines) check the plants about twice a day. Similar inspections in a retail supermarket would unearth the most stomach-turning practices. The state inspectors were quite thorough and businesslike in their duties in all the wholesale plants.

The federal inspectors in the Home Pride plant seemed even more thorough in their inspection. They checked to see that all equipment was cleaned immediately after use. Large hot water hoses with 200-degree water were used to clean each piece of equipment thoroughly. Very large drains were found in all the plants, unlike the situation in the supermarkets, which constantly have difficulty with garbage and putrid meat backing up in the drainage system because of inadequate care in construction planning. The federal inspectors made six in-plant inspections, some of which included walking through the entire plant.

One inspection is called the *AQL inspection*. This inspection scores the number of defects found in various areas. The score is based on the number of minor, major, and critical faults found on inspection. The defects checked for cover a wide range of items including hair, hair clusters, hide or wool, bone, blood clots, parasitic spots, types of parasites observed, bruise or injury, improper trim, paint flecks, rust, dirt, insects, feces—and the list goes on, covering most possibilities for contamination.

Another inspection check the day I was present included observation of boneless manufactured meat products. The USDA inspector checked beef, veal, and lamb, including briskets, shanks, flanks, chucks, plates, loins, rounds, and other items observed. The inspector checked fresh beef trimmings for bone fragments or improper trim. Because the bone barrel was placed too close to the trimming tub, one thin blade bone fell into the trimmings. The inspector found the bone. I have never seen a state inspector check any of these items in retail stores for such conditions.

What's Happening in Retail?

Thus far, Connecticut and many other states have not established anything for the retail level that is even near the inspection check list established for processing wholesale plants. I have found objects in hundreds of trimming tubs that could cause sickness and even death if ground and eaten. In 1968 I found pieces of a glass coffee cup that had fallen into the ground beef tub. Ground glass can kill. When you grind beef, you push the meat in very fast; consequently, you don't see many objects that pass into the mill head. You hear a popping and spitting noise when the object hits the blade, but this could be cartilage, bone, sinew, or almost anything. And on occasions it *is* almost anything.

The people who buy meat from retail markets—and that represents almost every man, woman, and child in the country—have no protection at all from this sort of risk. I found glass from unknown sources in ground meat on several occasions in 1961, 1963, 1964, 1967, 1968, and most recently in 1971. These dates cover experiences in three states and five different stores, four owned by two national chains and one an independent grocery chain. The names of the specific stores are not important, because such carelessness is happening all over the country. I cannot prove that these incidents took place because in each case it happened in a very few minutes and I had no camera available. The fact remains that such carelessness exists and the danger from this carelessness will continue unless the consumer is given the protection of even a small degree of the inspection presently found in processing plants today.

Some other objects found in ground beef tubs over the years from 1961 to 1971 include gum, cigarettes, plastic combs, boning knives, trash, hair, detergent, floor cleaner, nitrates, cardboard, both plastic and glass buttons, pieces of food trays, beer can tops, sunglasses, metal staples, employee name tags, and one prophylactic device. I hope that last item was merely a joke.

There is enough promiscuity in some retail meat departments to make similar stories in *Jungle* look like fairy tales. In 1961, while I was taking a frozen food inventory, I saw a meat manager and a meat wrapper unconcernedly making love on a meat block. In fact, there have been many love affairs observed in meat departments over the years. But the number of affairs is not the point—other working environments have them too. The point is, obviously, that meat blocks are no place for sex.

Wholesale Sanitation Checks

The wholesale sanitation check list is quite comprehensive: inspectors check pens, docks, floors, walls, drains, all equipment, lavatories, lighting, ventilation, storage areas, water supplies and even pest control. The inspectors check for personal hygiene of all employees, including personal habits, dress, disease and health hazards.

One employee at the plant forgot to wash his hands. The inspector reminded him. Another didn't have a hat on his head, although he was fast to put it on when the inspector came into the room. Next time you shop in your favorite supermarket, look for some of these things. Take a sheet of paper along and check all the things mentioned. See how many meat cutters aren't wearing hats or hair nets. See how many have cigarettes or cigars hanging out of their mouths, and then go on with your list from there.

I Wonder What Goes on Back There?

It's doubtful that any supermarkets will allow you to observe their cutting room or cooler unless they have just finished cleaning. The meat manager will try to give you a line like: "Our insurance doesn't cover customers in working areas," or "Company policy prohibits customers in the cutting room because they may contaminate the meat products." He will say, "This is for your protection—I'm sure you will understand," or "You wouldn't want just anyone walking through here whenever they pleased."

I have a friend who feels uneasy about restaurants because he worked for several while he was attending school. He is quite bold—before he eats in any restaurant, he rushes into the kitchen to see how sanitary the conditions are, and if the kitchen doesn't get his approval, he leaves. I feel the same way about meat departments.

None of the meat cutters I know ever buy from the meat case; they always cut their own. They *know* what goes on back there.

If customers by the thousands started asking for personal tours where they buy their meat, maybe the companies would start trying to maintain sanitary conditions.

This may be a good way to start changing conditions in this country if the present laws aren't extended down through retail supermarkets to give the public the protection it rightfully deserves.

The Wholesale Business Has Come a Long Way

The federal government is doing an excellent job inspecting interstate processors (processors shipping across statelines). They go to extremes on occasion, but it is for the protection of the public.

A good example of how careful and conscientious the federal inspectors are took place on August 27, 1971, in the Home Pride plant. The inspector and I were in his office, where he was filling out reports when the sausage maker came up for permission to pull the smoked and cooked frankfurters out of the cooking cabinet. We walked down to the cooking room, where the inspector very carefully checked the inside temperature of the meat before it was passed and okayed. The inspector checks all cooked and prepared meats, and they all must pass proper temperature checks or they are left in the cooker until the temperatures are right. All items that come in—including compounds for food products, pest control devices, cleaning solutions, and everything else that enters or leaves the plant—is subject to inspection or lab analysis. If there is any doubt about the product, they will double-check and wait for the lab report.

Before the plant is closed at night, the inspector checks all equipment to make sure it was cleaned properly. Retail meat departments would save money in the long run if they broke down all their equipment each night, cleaned the machines, and oiled them before the next operation. They would save money by cutting down on bacteria contamination and filth, which turn fresh meat dark very fast. They would also increase the service life of the machines. Any state or federal in-

112 / Meat Eaters are Threatened

spector will say the same thing. The companies know, but they are like old men, "set in their ways."

While many wholesale processing plants don't look as good as their retail counterparts on the outside, they have what it takes to do a good job on the inside. They are a half-century ahead of the retail supermarkets. They have done all they can to improve the standards, whereas the retail supermarkets have not only been negligent in this area, but at times, dishonest. This infuriates the wholesale packers, particularly since they have been subject to criticism, and the supermarkets have so far "gotten away with it." The wholesalers take great care to make sure that not even a single animal hair is left on the beef they process, because the federal and state inspectors go around with spotlights and magnifying glasses and count each hair with a special counting device. If they find one thing wrong, they start looking for something else, so the processor is constantly striving to do an excellent job to enhance his good record. Processors are striving for excellence, and many are close to reaching it, even though it seems an almost impossible goal in a business like this, because meat is a very delicate, highly perishable item involving many specialties and talents.

The wholesale processor can't even start his processing operation in the morning unless the federal inspector goes around and checks to see again if all equipment was cleaned properly the day before. If he finds something wrong, all operations are held up until the condition is rectified.

The wholesale industry has every right to be furious with the disparity between the wholesale and retail industries. Both are processing meat for human consumption and if any one of them should have strict surveillance and inspection, it should be the retailers. They are the last to handle the product before the consumer receives it.

Chapter VIII

THE GROSS PROFIT PICTURE

Every business from baseball and football to medicine and law has its "pros." In the meat business, however, the word may not be synonymous with respect. Sure, there are good guys who treat their help right, but these people don't merit much comment on the district or division level. Instead, you usually hear about the man who has the highest gross profit. These are the heroes of the quarter, the fiscal quarter of thirteen weeks. Companies may release their figures at different periods, but they all revere the man who sustains the highest gross. He becomes a symbol of success for many of the young, aggressive meat cutters who have their eyes on head meat cutter, meat manager, and future meat supervisor positions.

In the meat business it takes many talents to become successful. Those who make it big must be doing something right. But they must choose who to do right by—the company or the customer.

First listen to the overt propaganda that bombards everyday life in the business. It says, in effect, that *the customer is always right*. The customer shall receive the freshest product possible. The customer shall not be deceived by erroneous prices or incorrect weights on purchases. Many companies go one step further by saying, "We double your money back if you are not satisfied with the product." Still, the customer is caught in the middle.

The Companies Keep the Public in the Dark

The customer doesn't understand how to buy meat. The majority of customers are completely ignorant about the fantastic number of steaks, chops, and roasts. Many cannot even tell the difference between veal and pork cuts or even between pork and beef cuts, not to mention literally hundreds of items within one single line of meat, like beef. What is a shell steak? Where does it come from? Are Delmonicos, eye of rib, and Spencer steaks all the same thing? Where does the porterhouse steak come from?

Why is it that almost every company has different names for various cuts of meat? Why not make the cuts standard across the entire country so people know what they are buying? In the long run you are spending more money on food than you spend on your clothing, cars, and even your home.

Wouldn't it be nice if you could buy right for your family? Perhaps you are paying hundreds of dollars on cuts of meat which you are conditioned to think are the best buy. One example of this would be cold cuts, as compared to steaks. If you figure the price per pound of most lunch meat items, you will find you are paying as much or even more than you would pay per pound for good steak. But this is only part of the problem, and this is only one example of what they call meat merchandising.

You Can't Merchandise a Can of Beans?

You can't really merchandise a can of beans. You can change the price slightly, but most smart buyers know that beans are beans and that the store next door sells them for 2 cents less.

With meat, it's different. Let's take a beef short loin, which consists of the loin without the sirloin. The porterhouse and T-bone cuts are left to process. If this bulk slab of short loin is merchandised to its greatest potential, it would not just be cut into regular ¾-inch porterhouse and T-bone steaks. Instead, the same meat would be cut into some porterhouse and T-bones about ½-inch thick; they would be called "thin slice" porterhouse and T-bone steaks.

But shell steaks are also thin-cut T-bones. If you bought it—you paid from 10 to 20 cents a pound more for it than you would have paid for the ¾-inch steak. Had you bought the regular T-bone, you could have bought two cans of beans with your savings. But perhaps you wanted thin-cut steaks. If this is the case, why should you pay more per pound for a steak that is cut a quarter-inch thinner? The company justifies it by saying that there is more labor involved. Not really. Actually, you just helped the head meat cutter make "gross profit."

Perhaps you would like a real status symbol, so you decide to go first class and buy a Kansas City steak, or a New York strip steak, as it is called in the East. This time the store extends a little labor to take out the bone—and you are charged double price. Now if you have lots of money or if you need that status symbol, flash those beautiful boneless Kansas City steaks down on the checking counter. But if you don't have money to burn, you will buy the T-bone and have enough money for ten more cans of beans. This is part of the customers dilemma: the store merchandises a piece of meat, giving it a fancy name—instead of eye of rib, it is called a Spencer steak or a Delmonico. Unfortunately, it will sell. You may not know what it is, but it is red, it looks fresh, and it's higher-priced than the steak next to it, so it must be better. You buy it and you feel good about it; so what's wrong with that? Not a thing. You helped the meat cutter, the company, the city, the state, and even the Gross National Product of the country. But you should know what you're buying. It would be nice to know what you have just eaten. These are a few of the problems of the consumer.

Gross: Makes a Busy Man Happy

The smart meat manager, on the other hand, now must find the happy medium between what the company says and what it means. Many company policies turn out to be only a piece of paper.

I worked for many of the so-called pros in the business, the guys who could "cut a good gross." Most didn't make it by following stated company policy. There are hundreds of ways to make and lose gross. You can make gross if you have a number of "price leaders," like steaks at cost or below cost, advertised to bring in the customer. This is known as "baiting." The way you make gross here is to run out of those big sale items and hope they don't ask for "rain checks" on the item. The key here is that convincing smile on the meat cutter's face when he says, "We just ran out; we expect to have some more in the morning." Meanwhile, they have you captive, you need a few things anyway, and you decide he was pretty nice about the whole thing, so you buy some other items.

The August 1971 issue of *Consumer Reports* mentioned that the Federal Trade Commission looked at supermarket price advertising in Washington, D.C., San Francisco and Baltimore. In one survey of 137 stores, investigators found that 11 percent of advertised items were not available to the consumer. In a smaller sample, investigators found 9 percent of the items priced wrong. In "a very substantial majority of the instances," the price on the package was higher than the price in the newspaper. "In Washington alone, between 21 and 26 percent of the products advertised by most of the largest chains were out of stock or overpriced. Other investigators came up with similar results in St. Louis and Nassau County, N.Y." The unavailability or overpricing was reported to be twice as high in low-income areas in the cities sampled.[1]

Another way to make gross is to spend as much time as you can on merchandising and as little time as you can on cleaning up the market and fighting bacteria. Most of the stores have just about mastered both principles. I constantly learned new ways to make gross profit. Many of the stores were pushing as much bone and fat as they could get away with, without hurting sales. When steaks are on sale and really start to move, the word goes out, "Don't chime the bone," and "Easy on the trim." There is more profit in the boneless roast and steaks so they narrow the spread in the display case on bone-in roast and steaks and push the boneless items.

There is more profit in ground round than in ground chuck, but I found, in most cases, that there is *no difference* between ground round and ground chuck, except in the price. As I mentioned earlier in this book, ground round presumably is leaner than ground chuck. However, in most cases not only do you not get ground round exclusively, but you are also buying the same product sold as ground chuck. The store may change the food tray size to fool you.

Another common practice of some meat managers in the country is costing the American public millions of dollars each year. This practice made the news in an Associated Press release on March 21, 1973, when two Democratic Congressmen accused the Safeway food chain of cheating the public of millions of dollars each year by fraudulently labeling and pricing meat. The Congressmen, Benjamin Rosenthal of New York and Jerome Waldie of California cited such examples as club steaks sold as T-bone and chuck steak sold as rib steak. I personally witnessed this practice in the majority of the stores I worked in for ten years. This is a good way for a company to make easy money.

Little old ladies get angry when you want to save them money by trying to sell them ground chuck when no ground round is packaged. All the manager does is change the name-slug and the price on the automatic scale, and like magic they are happy again. Few people could bring happiness to the eyes of a little old lady that fast and easily—and it helps the gross. The same thing is true of beef liver and calf liver in many of the stores today. The stores buy beef livers, cut the large end up for beef livers, skin the small end, slice it thin, and call it calf liver.

Remember that chuck roast you gave the butcher and told him to bone out and grind into ground chuck? Well, there is a good chance that your chuck roast is now a boneless chuck roast which will be sold to someone else for more money. The butcher may just grind up some lean trimmings from the ground beef tubs. This helps the gross.

This practice is followed most often with stew meat. The procedure is to tear off the price tag, grind some lean trimmings, put the tag on, and give it back to the customer. Meanwhile, the original stew meat goes sailing down the conveyor line to be rewrapped.

On May 31, 1973, *The Daily Democrat,* a Woodland-Davis, California newspaper, carried a story about a Washington meat cutter who came forth to explain some of the terrible things he did as a meat cutter for thirty-five years while working for a major chain; Andrew Grady "has a long list of tricks that have been used over the years by management to dupe or fleece the shopper. The alert citizen knows the minefield he walks through, but Grady says he sees few of these alert ones."[2]

Oh! That Inventory Control

There are other factors involved in the gross profit picture, including inventory control and product rotation. Inventory control is simple. If you order too much product, you end up with overage and your gross profit may be hurt. If you don't order enough, you may lose customers and volume sales. So you try to order the right amount and merchandise it to its potential.

Most stores rotate their merchandise in the meat case according to a timetable. An example of this would include the prescribed maximum allowable time which various types of meats may be left in the case according to company policy, city laws and state laws. Ground beef, ground chuck, ground round, and meat loaf may have a one-day case-life as far as the company is concerned. Fresh red meat items may have a three-day case-life, chickens and poultry two days, smoked meats ten days. The fresh dating system for each company is difficult for many employees to remember and is totally confusing to the customer. But when the employee figures it out, he pulls out the outdated meats and they become known as "reworks." Reworks usually are handled on Monday and Thursday mornings. The dark steaks, if they aren't too dark, are put back out or reprocessed into cube steaks. The roast may be "faced up" by cutting a thin slice off the top or maybe reprocessed into stew or cubes or in some cases, steaks.

Much of the reworks from beef items will be boned out and placed in ground beef. The reworks should be ground that day, but many stores are careless and mix reworks with their fresh trim. In this case they may go for days before they are ground, and the bacteria build-up from the older meat causes all the meat to turn bad.

Once again, because of gross profit, the store must consider whether to dump the bad meat out or to grind it—the decision depends on the individual. I have seen supervisors dump entire bone barrels on top of the meat blocks to check for meat being thrown away.

Pork Sausages: A High-Profit Item

The pork items are also checked the same way, but with pork you must be very careful. Rotten pork could kill you. Some pork, if it is questionable, will be boned out and made into pork cutlets. If there is doubt that the item will last the day, it is put into the sausage trimmings.

Many stores grind their own sausage. Some do not because of lack of universal recipes for all stores. Sausage grinding should be left to the packing houses and processing plants, where there is good federal and state inspection and control.

I have lost count of the number of times that a meat cutter has said, "Boy, this pork is overripe; it had better find a home soon." What is usually done when the meat is rotten and slimy is to add a couple more packages of sausage seasoning.

Another reason for being disgusted with food stores that grind sausage is that they traditionally see this as a gross profit item, so they really push it by pumping tremendous amounts of fat into the grind.

Whatever the stores can't sell to the general public because it looks, smells, and is rotten, they freeze and sell to local restaurants or other special customers. As I described in Chapter V, this is a common practice for many supermarkets.

Temperature Control Is Important

How can you preserve something that is already dead? To put it in simpler terms, a process of decomposition starts to take place as soon as the animal is killed.

Meat therefore must be handled very carefully and kept under ideal temperature controls to retard decomposition. About 32 to 48 degrees Fahrenheit in the cutting room would be acceptable. If you have an efficient dating and rotating system, you would have a chance of sustaining a fresh product for the customer, plus maintaining a good gross profit for the company. Unfortunately, most of the markets are kept at temperatures around 42 to 68 degrees. This is not an acceptable temperature range for holding down the growth of bacteria. Most of the stores lose some case-life on meats by temperature alone. After the meat is cut and placed on a conveyor line, it may sit there exposed to the air, light, and heat in the cutting room for several minutes to sometimes two to six hours. This causes the meat to shrink and turn dark. This darkening of meat, caused by its oxidation, is speeded up by any one of the factors mentioned. When all of these factors of heat, light, and air are combined, oxidation increases so that you may end up with a dark steak before it reaches the meat case. If these factors are not controlled, the meat case-life is shortened considerably. When you pick that steak out and take it home, it may stay fresh for a very short period of time. This problem is not as widespread in the packing houses, because the federal and state controls make sure that proper temperature ranges are maintained. But very little is ever said to any meat manager who makes a good "gross" as long as the company doesn't catch him doing something wrong.

After working for scores of meat managers over the years, I feel it is obvious that management closes its eyes to many wrongs as long as they add to the gross profit. Andrew Grady, the Washington meat cutter mentioned earlier, feels these conditions exist because of a lack of supervision in the industry.[3]

122 / Meat Eaters are Threatened

CHAPTER IX

WEIGHTS AND MEASURES—HA!

The year is 1967 and I'm working in a number of different stores in both Missouri and Kansas, wherever the company needs me most. One store in Kansas City, Missouri, in a predominantly black neighborhood, was cheating the customers. Chickens were on sale for 25 cents a pound. This was below cost, so the head meat cutter left a metal stapler on the automatic scale while he weighed.

The chickens weren't the only "price leader" that week, nor were they the only item on which he gypped the customers on weight. The same thing happened each week on all price leaders. One week it would be steaks, T-bone, porterhouse and sirloin. The customers thought they were reaping tremendous savings, and most went away with a smile. The great majority of customers never knew they were cheated.

An elderly lady picked out three nice steaks and looked up at the boss with poor suffering eyes and said, "Are these nice steaks? My son-in-law is coming in from Texas this weekend. I don't have much money, but nothing is too good for my daughter and her husband. Maybe you could pick me out some?" The head meat cutter, reaching down in the case and picking out three T-bone steaks, said, "You don't want those—these have less waste—don't you want to save money?" The steaks he had picked out had the wrong weight and price because a metal stapler had been deliberately left on the scale at the time of pricing. That lady and hundreds of other good, steady customers were being taken in a very deceitful way that is close to impossible to detect. Customers were cheated anywhere from 20 cents to $2 per package, depending on the price and weight of the meat purchased.

The metal stapler weighed 10 ounces, but if you had brought one of those steaks home and had weighed it on your home scale, you might have thought you had gotten a better bargain. Most home scales will not weigh accurately. They're probably off from 1 to 3 pounds, so there is very little chance of detecting a 10-ounce mistake in weight.

One customer did pull a sneaky trick on the head meat cutter. She picked out four large sirloin steaks and took them up to the front of the store and weighed them on the produce scale. When she came back, she headed for me, saying "I'm telling you meat prices are high enough—but you people are something else." All the customers looked at us, and I felt it would be interesting to see how the head meat cutter would handle the matter, so I rang the meat bell.

He came right out with a phony smile on his face, and said, "What's wrong, sweety?"

She said, "Come on, now, what's going on back there? Why can't you get the right weight on these steaks? Are you chasing your meat wrapper around the scale? You know, if I wasn't a steady customer—"

He broke in and said, "Look, you know I'd do anything for you. I even offered to bring some steaks over to your house personally one night, but you said the old man was home. You know how hard it is to break in a new girl."

She said, "Just like I thought, hanky-panky."

He said, "Now, you know I'm not like that. Give me those steaks; I'm going to straighten this new girl out, right now."

This was hard to believe. Of all the people who bought meat from the store, the one person who caught the deliberate mistake was apparently not even concerned about the $2 blunder; she seemed to be looking for a flirtation.

The head meat cutter did get caught on the next chicken sale. It seems that the larger weights like hams, large roasts, and turkeys were never suspected for wrong weights. The single bagged chickens were his downfall because the weight was quite low and the customers in this neighborhood purchased chickens quite often in other stores, so there were a few people who did find the error. It's doubtful that anyone called the state weights and measures inspector to complain. They did, however, ask the head meat cutter about the erroneous price and weight. He simply told the customers the girl forgot to set the right tare weight. No one really seemed to indicate that the mistakes were intentional. This practice went on for years without any let-up.

The second man in charge in the market wasn't pleased with the way the head meat cutter did business, but this job was located close to his home and he wanted to keep it that way. If the gross profit falls, the company usually ships you out to another store and brings in a new crew—with new ideas.

Weights and Measures Do Affect Gross Profit

The bad thing about a head meat cutter or meat manager who cheats on weights is that if he ever stops cheating, it will show up in his gross profit. Suppose a head meat cutter maintains a gross profit of 26 percent, which was a good gross in 1967. If he starts overcompensating for price leaders by adding additional weight to purchases, or setting the tare weight indicator above the zero level, and if he does this consistently over a period of one year, it shows a pattern of four quarters of high gross. If the other head meat cutters aren't cheating in exactly the same manner, their gross profit should be lower, say from 18 to 23 percent. Most gross profit figures will not remain consistent each quarter; instead, they will vary because of inventory overage, excessive reworks, and hundreds of minor mistakes. The man who cheats excessively will remain higher in the same classified distribution range, and although he may fluctuate from 25 to 28 percent, he is ahead of the pack and is making friends with the supervisor and the district office, and in time is making friends within other districts of the division. When he stops cheating on tare weight altogether, his gross profit picture will change drastically, causing him to plummet to the bottom of the list.

The company district supervisor will make a special trip to see what happened. He will spend many hours snooping around for the wrong reasons, never suspecting the real reason. Instead, he will criticize poor inventory control, reworks, shrinkage due to premature or excessive breaking down of forequarter and hindquarter beef, profit negligence in cutting, or poor ratio in profit items. If all else fails, they accuse the help of stealing meat, or the part-time checkers are accused of ringing meat items on the grocery key.

No one wants to know how the man makes a high gross profit. It's always, "I don't know what he's doing, but he's doing something right." But let that same man come up with a couple of bad inventories and watch the criticism. In most cases the man with the low gross profit is the man dealing most fairly with the consumer. However, he will soon be out of a job, moved to another store, and broken in rank and salary to a journeyman meat cutter.

There are hundreds of ways of making money off customers without their knowing. One of them is by weight. Remember the old joke about the meat cutter with his finger on the scale while weighing? That practice will not usually work because "platform scales" show number deviation from the slightest muscle movement in your arm. The customer watches the meat cutter weigh the chicken or other meat from the back side of the scale through a small window on the scale. It's almost impossible to cheat on the new computerized automatic scales this way because they are so sensitive. Even a few hundredths of a pound deviation will cause the scale to refuse weight disclosures. The new automatic scales break the pound down into 100 calibrations, so a chicken weighing 2½ pounds would register 2.50. Therefore, to cheat, you must either place a stationary object like a metal stapler on the scale weighing surface or turn back the tare weight indicator dial.

The platform scale used for weighing special orders is manipulated differently. In many cases the customers are watching the meat cutter weigh, for example, a chicken. They usually see that the scale is set on zero, but if the meat cutter is fast, he will catch the scale weight when it bounces to its peak level. This is when the customer should say, "Let me see how much it weighs," without taking the cutter's word. Don't get the impression that every meat cutter is cheating the public on weight—this is far from the truth. Most are honest, but when the company threatens him because of a low gross profit, he may resort to cheating on weight. I have seen it in many stores over the years.

The Hand is Quicker than the Eye

One very old trick used years ago that is still being used in some markets in the country shows American ingenuity at its best, but used for a wrong purpose.

The meat manager places a small wood or cardboard box containing sawdust on the floor under the platform scale. A customer decides she would like a nice fryer for chicken cacciatore, so she asks the meat cutter to pick her out a nice one. He goes back into the cooler and picks out a fryer, brings it out and tells the customer how nice it is. She asks how much it weighs. While the cutter was talking, he did the old sleight of hand trick and put a small lead sinker (the kind used for fishing, usually) in the anal section of the chicken. He throws the chicken on the scale, stands back with his hands spread out, and says, "Only $2.37 and that's a beauty, good color; and we just got them in this morning." When he picks the chicken up, he holds the bottom down behind the scale and the weight falls out, landing in the sawdust without a sound.

What Happened to Inspection?

Good meat inspection could stop these and many other fraudulent practices that take place in the retail meat business today. The problem is that inspection occurs in a store perhaps once every six months or once a year. In some stores, inspection may be delayed for three years. When inspectors do come in, they spot-check perhaps a dozen packages from the meat case from among thousands of packages, many of which are frequently off in weight or price or both. They check the scale for accuracy, but as I mentioned earlier, there is nothing wrong with the machine; it is gross profit that encourages devious methods of changing the weight. Before they leave, they attach an inspection tag on the scale showing that the scale was inspected and found to be in good working order. This type of inspection is good, but it should take place more often, and it should include a larger sample.

Many stores in this country turn their tare weight indicator above zero on Saturdays because they know that the state inspectors are off duty that day.

Some other observed ways of deceiving the public on

fair weights includes coffee cups left on the scale while weighing, flat metal plates placed on the scale surface and sometimes another package item left there while weighing.

The consumer is being taken for a ride by many retail meat establishments, both large and small.

Watch Them When They Cut Your Side Order

Watch out when you buy your special side of beef of sale. There have been occasions when the meat manager has taken a few steaks from the customer's special order, priced them, and put them in the meat case. This is a good way to help his gross profit. Let's suppose the side of beef weighed 300 pounds, and let's say he took 10 pounds of steaks from various parts of the side order. To replace the weight, he probably took some ground beef trimming from a tub and gave you 10 more pounds of ground beef.

Inaccurate weighing and bait-and-switch operations are perpetrated against the public daily. Be especially careful of the misleading advertised bulk-meat bargains and freezer-meat bargains. For example the FTC Consumer Bulletin No. 5 documented this typical case. Two Maryland women answered an advertisement for beef at only 32 cents a pound. The women were convinced by the operator that the meat was not fit for their families. The operator talked the women into buying 740 pounds of beef for $580 or more than 78 cents a pound. He assured them there would be no more than ten percent waste. This was absurd because the USDA estimates the average side order of beef will yield about 50 percent edible meat and 50 percent bone and waste. When the packaged meat was delivered, they found they had about 385 pounds. Keep in mind that even bulk weight had fat and bone.

Maybe Things Will Get Better—Someday?

A survey conducted in May of 1963 by the National Bureau of Standards, according to *Consumer Reports,* said that 80 percent of all prepackaged foods were under their specified weights.[1]

The criteria for weights and measures for the states are derived from the National Bureau of Standards. The law providing for inspection was approved by the Congress of the United States on June 14, 1836.

Congressional hearings from 1963 to 1966 led by Senator Philip A. Hart finally made possible the passage of the Fair Packaging and Labeling Act in 1966.

The law is weak and diluted. It merely prohibits misleading labels and states that ingredients and package sizes must be clearly displayed. Some organizations, including Grocery Manufacturers of America (GMA) and the National Association of Manufacturers (NAM), tried to fight this truth-in-packaging bill. The GMA organized a special committee to fight the bill. As a result, the provisions on weights and measures were not embodied into the law. That is what the American public has to live with. There is an unholy alliance which works within the system to prevent or dilute similar laws.

CHAPTER X

LET'S HOPE WE DON'T BECOME WHAT WE EAT

Lucretius lived from 99 B.C. to 55 B.C. and though it may seem a short period compared to modern life spans, he was trying to tell us something: *Quod ali ci-*

bus est aliis fiat acre veneum—What is food to one man may be a fierce poison to another. The Roman poet may have looked at our destiny more than 2,000 years ago and prophesied the fate of modern man.

Dr. Harvey W. Wiley, who was the first director of the Food and Drug Administration, felt there was reason for concern about the destiny of man's health because of what he ate. In 1902 Wiley established a special group of volunteer employees from the Department of Agriculture, who were called "Dr. Wiley's Poison Squad." It was the intention of the Poison Squad to try to determine how man was affected by the number of additives and preservatives put in food.

Dr. Wiley chose strong, healthy men for the tests, because he felt they would have maximum resistance to the harmful effects of adulterated food. The theory behind this was that if the men showed danger signs from the specified period of exposure, then it would be assumed that the effect would be greater in young children and elderly persons.

The men ate and drank only those foods prepared by the department's kitchen. Six of the twelve volunteers were given a normal diet with the addition of the most commonly used food preservative of the time—boric acid. The other six men were given a normal diet with sodium borate (borax) included. The study concluded that when both borax and boric acid are constantly introduced into the diet in small doses over a long period, or over short periods in large doses, the individual's digestion and health are affected and there are disturbances in the appetite. These were crude tests in the feeble beginning of food science. Since that time, now over seven decades later, many poisonous substances have found their way into man's meat dish.

Colleges, boarding schools, and other institutions have put saltpeter in vegetables, meats, and potatoes with the belief that it would slow down the sex drive.

Saltpeter can cause stomach distress, nausea, vomiting, and excessive urine discharges.

Dr. Wiley in his famous *Bulletin 84* on Food Adulteration, stated that saltpeter affects the gonads and causes harmful effects in men. He refused permission for its use in cured meats.[1]

Boric acid is still used by small processing plants in the country to keep "skippers" (small flies) off the hams during processing. The FDA considers boric acid a poison and warns that it should not be introduced into food items.

Fish is sometimes placed in ice containing preservatives, including sodium benzoate, sodium nitrite, hydrogen peroxide, and chlorine; none of these preservatives are truly safe and if used in excess they can kill.

The FDA has initiated some steps to stop the use of chlortetracycline in poultry (and fish products). They are also halting the use of oxytetracycline in poultry.[2] The tetracyclines are antibiotics which are used to prolong the shelf life of a product far beyond the normal period of freshness. The chickens are dipped in a solution before shipment to supermarkets. This practice is still going on, and it raises a question in the minds of people like myself. Can a "fresh" chicken twenty-one days old really be considered fresh? From a meat cutter's point of view, I would prefer to abstain from eating that chicken.

Almost every cold cut or lunch meat item has an entry written on the package disclosing what ingredients are included. Two usual chemicals used in cold meats are sodium nitrate and sodium nitrite. These chemicals fix and hold and even enhance the natural color of meat products. One of the many potential dangers involved in using these in meats is that it covers up the real condition of the meat. Meat may be rancid but the rancidity is hidden.

The list of chemical poisons used in meat products is

quite long and of little value to a reader unless he is a chemist, toxicologist, biochemist, or food scientist. Some experts may say a chemical is not poison when it is used in very small, carefully administered amounts. They may compare and say that anything could kill you in excess, water, for instance, or salt. This may be true; however, how many people have died in the last fifty years from eating too much salt or drinking too much water? The National Institutes of Health have for some time now voiced their strong feelings against the use of sodium nitrite in foods. The stomach is affected by sodium nitrite, and it is converted into nitrous acid, which affects a variety of lower organisms. In 1973 it was disclosed that sodium nitrate also used in most lunch meats was found to be one of the worst carcinogens known to man.

After realizing Americans' enormous propensity to consume meat as a major source of protein, it is obvious that meat eaters are threatened.

Consumer Reports in August 1971, reported that Americans eat 11.3 billion pounds of ground beef in a year. This is about half the beef consumption in the United States.[3] The 1970 *Statistical Abstract* from the federal government indicates that civilian per capita consumption of meats (carcass weight) in 1969 was 181.1 pounds. Beef consumption per capita was 109.7 pounds, veal 3.3 pounds, lamb and mutton 3.4 pounds, and pork (excluding lard) was 64.7 pounds.[4] The *National Livestock Producer* published an article which was restated in the book, *The Poisons in Your Food* by William Longgood. It said that if the average American can survive the life expectancy of about sixty-eight years, he will consume the meat equivalent of 33 hogs, 10 lambs, 8 steers and 4 veal calves.[5] A scholarly study by the American Meat Institute disclosed that all the frankfurters eaten by Americans this year would stretch to the moon and back, and there would be enough left

Let's Hope We Don't Become What We Eat / 133

over to encircle the earth five times, like a chain of satellites; in less fanciful terms, Americans eat 5.5 billion frankfurters a year.[6] Longgood's book also mentions that animals used for meat are subjected to much use of chemicals and argues that meat is the most thoroughly tampered-with item in the American diet.[7]

Lunch meat items are injected with chemicals before the consumer purchases the meat. Curing processes, coloring, flavoring materials, emulsifiers, preservatives, refining agents, and bleaching all constitute further *legal* adulteration of meat products. But the unknown abuses which take place after the meat leaves the packing house really only start when it is received by the retail meat establishment. These abuses run the gamut from simple little household means of making the ground beef look red by mixing paprika in the grind to full-fledged unscrupulous acts against the public. The *Consumer Reports* 1971 study[8] did not find illegal preservatives or color holders to make the meat stay red, but they *are* being used, although to a lesser extent than they were ten or twenty years ago, thanks to a special test made in the supermarkets by the state inspectors.

There is another practice which some of the small stores use: they place red spotlights over the meat case. This practice, while not as serious an offense as others, is unfair because the consumer looks at the meat under the red lights, thinking it is bright and fresh, and only finds out when she gets home that the pork chops are greenish gray in color. Most of the major food chains are using a new spotlight which has a slight blue cast. This light is not as harsh on the meat as a white spotlight; it makes meat packages look crisp and fresh.

It may not be a bad idea to look at the meat lights used where you shop. If the store is using red lights, make your own judgment about whether use of those lights constitutes a fair consumer practice.

Unlike using red lights to make meat appear fresher, chemical additives may have a longer lasting effect on the human body. Some additives cause derangements in the function of the human metabolism. Most take years of exposure to cause alterations in the biological structure of the body, but there are subtle effects. Trained pathologists could detect some early signs of the effects of additives because some vital organs become enlarged.

Some observed signs have been seen in animal tests over the years which show enlarged kidneys, livers, and spleens. Chemical additives in food are known to impede the normal functions of the vitamins and enzymes in the body. Medical experts over the past fifty years have suggested that many of the chemical food additives may lead to diseases of the body because of vitamin and enzyme deficiencies.

Some of the chemical additives that cause enzyme destruction include sodium nitrate, food dyes, sulphur dioxide, fluorides used in water processing, pesticides, and certain antibiotics and hormones used in the food production chain.

I became interested in chemical food additives and food-borne illnesses while working for my bachelor of science degree at Central Missouri State College long before I attended graduate school. Although my areas of concentration in college were speech, public relations, radio and television, communications, and business, this didn't stop me from reading every book, Senate subcommittee hearing, and magazine I could find on the subject.

America—and other countries—are not really sure what effects prolonged exposure to food additives will have upon the human body. The risk of two kinds of effects must still be determined. *Mutagenic effects* damage cells; this type of damage could be passed down through heredity to future generations. The other effects, which have already been discussed, cause damage to the body in a single generation through prolonged exposure. These are referred to as *teratogenic effects*. The FDA in recent years has taken it on itself to investigate mutagenic effects of food additives. This is a costly operation to the taxpayers, but it must be done.

When questions were raised through tests about the possible harmful effects of cyclamates, they were banned from sale or use in foods. Questions about other additives include some which are suspected of causing cancers, and others suspected of causing problems when they combine with still other chemicals in the body. These and many other problems exist which can be resolved only through legislation and research.

The Pure Food and Drug Act of 1906 required that our food supply be safe. The Food, Drug and Cosmetic Act of 1938 gave the government the power to enforce the regulations. But for over twenty years the public watched the government try to stop the fast, unending growth of additives in all types of foods without much hope of catching up. Now, since the 1960 amendment to the law, manufacturers must first prove that a color additive is safe before the FDA allows its use.

In addition, President Nixon presented a consumer message on October 30, 1969, asking that the G.R.A.S. list ("generally recognized as safe" for the intended purpose) be fully reviewed and revised where necessary to protect the consumer. This list includes additives many of which have a long safety record, including items like vinegar, baking powder, ascorbic acid, and many others.

Most food additives are harmless, perhaps even many of those which are considered poison if taken in large doses. Because of the very small additive mixture of these chemicals, the public may feel more at ease today than in years past. But this doesn't discount the fact that some additives that were thought to be safe at one time were later found to cause serious damage to humans. For this reason the government must continue its relentless investigations of all additives.

CHAPTER XI

COMMENTS AND RECOMMENDATIONS

There are no reasons why the conditions that exist in the retail meat business today should continue. If there are some who say the conditions aren't really bad, they are blind or have worked in a limited number of stores and states.

The fact remains that the retail meat business has not changed for the better. The stores have not kept up with the available modern improvements in the areas of health and sanitation. They are becoming progressively worse in their lack of concern for employees' safety and the public's health. The inspection of retail supermarkets has been hampered by inadequate funds and a shortage of skilled manpower.

What Can the States Do?

It is obvious that the states are having some difficulty inspecting both wholesale intrastate processing plants and all other establishments, including bake shops. Other consumer items that do not get enough attention are nonalcoholic beverages, frozen desserts, other frozen foods, cider and apple juice, oleomargerine, kosher foods, apples, potatoes and eggs. Frozen food lockers and coin-operated food and beverage machines also suffer from some degree of negligence.

The list may be larger or smaller, depending on the

state. The FDA is responsible for this inspection throughout the United States. The states are hard-pressed to do the job; presently they are the only real safeguard, because local health departments are ineffective.

The 1967 Meat Inspection Act provided a safeguard for the consumers' protection. If the states didn't bring their intrastate plants up to the federal meat inspection standards, the federal government would take over the inspection to protect the consumer. The act established a federal-state cooperative program with technical assistance and financial aid up to 50 percent of the total cost of the state's meat inspection program.

By the enactment and wording of the 1967 law, the federal government disclosed that the states were not doing a good enough job in protecting the consumer. If the federal government and the states want to really protect the consumer, they would worry about inspection in the retail supermarkets where almost every American must buy his meat. Most wholesale plants in this country receive more inspections in one week than the average supermarket receives in a year. Why is there so much disparity between the two businesses? The main reason, once again, is that the states are short of manpower and money. They spread limited numbers of inspectors between the wholesale intrastate plants and all other food establishments.

Instead of having the federal government financing half the programs and the states half, why not let the federal government take care of all inspection of intrastate wholesale plants instead of making the states bring their standards up to the federal level? USDA inspection will give the public the protection they deserve. The best way to get the quality of federal inspections is to have federal inspections. Everyone would benefit. The consumer would have exactly what the federal government proposes in the Wholesome Meat

Act and it would be done by the most competent inspection division, the U. S. Department of Agriculture. Most experts will agree that the USDA Inspection is far superior to other inspection systems.

The states would be benefited because they would not have the burden of intrastate plant inspection. All their inspectors could be used to inspect retail supermarkets and other required establishments. The states would save millions of dollars because they would not need to pay the 50 percent financial cost in maintaining a very expensive accelerated inspection program to meet federal standards. This savings is desperately needed because many states are in financial trouble. Part of the savings could go toward building a good inspection system for retail establishments.

What Can the Consumer Do Now?

Write to your congressman and explain that you feel it is time to protect the consumer where it really counts. It doesn't make sense to have the good inspection at each step of processing except at the most important step—the retail supermarket. All other inspections may be wasted, because meat cutters final-process the great majority of all meat items. When beef leaves the watchful eye of the USDA inspector, there is seldom even a hair present on the hindquarters, but when the retail supermarket finishes its mishandling of the beef, the USDA inspection is made worthless to the consumer.

What the Consumer Ought to Know

Watch when you buy meat in a supermarket. Many markets advertise USDA Choice meats but do not always receive a total shipment of choice beef. Most national food chains are usually an exception; they try to use choice at all times.

Don't be led astray by the fancy names that the supermarkets attach to the beef as private labels—super goody, super excellent, supreme, landcaster brand, super right, tender best, tender-ay—the list goes on to include every superlative in the English language.

Know the U. S. Department of Agriculture grades, because you need every bit of protection you can find. Make sure you're not paying for a higher priced grade than you're receiving The grades of beef include:

U.S. Grade Prime—the best quality, the best flavor, and the most tender and juicy, with good fat distribution (marbling) through the lean meat. It's also the most expensive.

U.S. Grade Choice—high quality. This is the grade sold in most retail stores. It is produced in such large amounts that it is often a very good buy. USDA Choice steaks and roasts will be tender and juicy. Choice beef also has good flavor.

U.S. Grade Good—has less marbling (marbling is what makes a steak more tender). You're better off with U.S. Good meats for ground beef dishes. U.S. Good beef is not as juicy and flavorful as the higher grades.

U.S. Grade Standard—has a mild flavor and lacks marbling to any extent. The beef will be relatively tender, but dry. This usually comes from still fairly young animals, about four years old. This beef would not be good cooked out over an open fire, but it would still be a buy for meat dishes cooked in a pressure cooker.

U.S. Grade Commercial—by far the leanest and the lowest priced grade. Meat without marbling lacks flavor, and in the case of U.S. Commercial meat, you would find very little tenderness.

The consumer should know that it's the price per serving that really counts, not the price per pound. Usually you can get four servings per pound of lean, boneless meat, and about two servings per pound of bone-in meat.

Buy a small manual or electric meat grinder; it's worth the money. Purchase a large chuck roast, a center cut to get leaner meat, then take it home and learn to bone it out for ground chuck. Invest about $2 in a boning knife—you won't be sorry.

Buy your chickens whole and learn to cut them up. Ask the meat cutter to break the corner of the bag, so you can smell the chicken, and see if it's fresh. This will save you some embarrassment and time. The meat markets sell large frying chickens for roasting at 10 cents a pound more than they charge for smaller fryers. Tell the meat cutter you want a 2½-3 pound fryer. Don't pay roasting chicken price for a fryer.

In the long run you can save more money on specials than you can buying a quarter or side of beef because of the waste on beef orders.

If you can afford an upright freezer, you will save by buying meat specials whenever available for your family.

You can save 20 or 30 cents a pound on stew meat if you buy boneless chuck roast and cut your own stew meat.

Buy rib steak instead of club steak. It's the same thing with the bone in it, and it will be a 60 to 80-cent a pound saving for your own family.

When you are looking for a tender sirloin steak, don't buy the first cut with the small bone. Always buy the sirloin with the long flat bone.

Be very careful when buying lunch meat, especially

a store's own brand of pre-packaged meat. Many times these meats are just old or outdated brands from the packer which the supermarket has re-labeled and re-wrapped. In the case of lunch meats, stay with brand names and you won't be sorry.

Don't buy cube steaks or minute steaks from the retail supermarket unless you don't mind paying for sinew tissue, or "seamation," as it is referred to in the trade. This is impossible to chew. Buy a cheap metal meat tenderizer for 69 cents and make your own high-quality cube steaks from center-cut round roast.

Don't buy homemade pork sausage made by the supermarket. If it's a national packer, USDA-inspected, go ahead and buy. You can make excellent sausage at a reasonable price if you buy boneless pork butts. A very simple sausage formula includes fresh pork, salt, pepper, and ground sage (rubbed). Run this through the meat grinder (fine plate) one time, add a little buttermilk or water for moisture, and then mix by hand. Season to your smell, *but do not eat any of the pork raw because it may have trichina worms.*

Don't buy packages that are torn open. Don't buy fresh meats that are not under refrigeration.

Don't buy calf liver unless it appears to be much lighter in color than the beef liver. Many markets sell the small lobe of the beef liver for calf liver.

If the liver is labeled "beef liver" and it has a texture like "pig skin," take it back unless you prefer being deceived on both price and product. They sold you pork liver.

For years supermarkets have sold lamb breasts with the fat taken off for lamb spareribs at a much higher cost. When buying lamb make sure it is firm, pink in color with a fine texture.

Much lamb goes un-inspected so make sure it has the USDA stamp on it. It's wise to squeeze a boneless pork butt to check it for firmness because the butts tend to be very fat.

Before you buy a roast with a strange name like "Watermelon roast" or "Bolder Gem" find out what it really is.

Slab bacon is less expensive and should stay fresh longer than presliced bacon. Slab bacon may be sliced and eaten either with the rind on or off.

If you buy some meat and find it's rotten, take it back and ask for double your money back if that is in their customer policy.

Never buy frozen fish from a fresh meat case, because this usually means it is put back in the freezer each night and then placed back in the fresh meat case the next day. Be careful of some frozen fish items in the freezer case. Much of the breaded fish has more breading than fish today. This is also true of many of the frozen beef steak varieties.

When buying fresh fish, try to buy as close to the source as possible. If that isn't convenient, check the scales; see if they cling to the body. Make sure the gills are reddish and the flesh firm and elastic. The eyes should be bright and bulging, not receded and glassy. Most important of all, smell the fish for any strong odor.

Before cooking or eating any meat, smell it—it's better to be safe than sorry.

If you buy several rib eye steaks and find that two are tender and juicy and easy to cut, while the others are tough, sinewy and lacking in flavor, they may have slipped you a couple of steaks from the chuck to help the gross profit.

Meat Deli Check List

Be very careful when you buy any food from any meat department delicatessen. You would be safer buying your cold cuts prepackaged from USDA-inspected national packers. But if you prefer the variety or taste found in a delicatessen, watch for these warning signs of lack of concern for health and sanitation. They may be an indication of even more serious things unknown to you.

Are the slicing machines free from clinging meat on metal surfaces?
Are there flies or evidence of insect and rodent contamination?
Is the meat you buy from the meat deli or meat department placed directly on the scale surface instead of on protective paper?
Are the food handlers smoking? Saliva from cigars or cigarettes causes contamination.
Are garbage containers open and exposed? Is there trash present?
Do the employees have on clean uniforms? Are they wearing protective hats to keep hair out of prepared foods?
Are the employees coughing, spitting or sneezing near food?
Are salads, desserts, and meat items covered and under refrigeration?
Are the deli pans and utensils clean?
Are the floors clean?
Are the counters clean?
Do the employees have sores on their hands that aren't properly bandaged with a clean bandage? Do the employees' hands appear to be clean?

If you can't answer most of these questions with the right answer, good luck. Earlier chapters explained some of the daily adulterations which take place in meat delicatessens and which may cause sickness or death.

Frozen Food Check List

Check to make sure products are not placed above the load level line in the frozen food case.

Make sure the thermometer in the case registers zero degrees or below. The thermometer cable runs down below the food so it will be colder than the frozen food.

Unlike fresh meat in many cases, the fresher frozen food items will be close to the top of the freezer case because employees don't like to reach down in the bottom of the freezer. It freezes their hands and they feel no real need to rotate this food because the old and new packages look the same, usually. Many retail companies don't date frozen food items. Some remain in the case for several years.

Check the temperature and condition of all packages. Were they left in the cardboard boxes, or are the individual packages placed in the case? The cycle of air movement can be easily impeded, causing packages to thaw out. The package should be solid, with no material adhering to the outside. Does it appear that the package leaked at one time?

Check precooked frozen foods for odor and appearance after they are defrosted to determine quality. This may reflect negligence in processing because of slow freezing, thawing, and refreezing.

Look for excessive dehydration in the products. Do they appear dry? If there is a bleached surface, it may mean improper packaging, temperature variance, or extremely long periods of freezing.

When to Buy

Monday morning is usually not a good time to buy, although many people probably think products would be fresher then. This is not true. Monday is the worst time to get a guarantee of freshness because much of the fresh meat items from the previous week are put back out after being trimmed or rewrapped.

The first of the week is slow, so many reworks will lay around in the case until Wednesday.

The best time to shop is from Wednesday to Saturday morning for the best prices, fresher products and the greatest selections.

Late Saturday night is a bad time to shop because many packages have been torn open and picked over, leaving a very poor selection. You may not even find the bargains you were looking for that night.

Where to Buy

If there is a processing plant near your home which is state or federally inspected and provides both wholesale and retail outlets, this would be the safest place to buy for your family. You would also save on price on many items.

Be very careful of the small beef outlets around the country who advertize special "beef bundles," and "side orders." If you buy there, make sure you are not paying for a better grade of beef than you receive. Many of these meat outlets sell all grades down to the lowest grade, Commercial.

The following is taken from a meat ad in the *Hartford Courant*. Similar ads appear in almost every newspaper across the country.

FREEZER MEATS

BUY NOW! SPECIAL MANAGER'S SALE

CHARGE IT! 90 DAYS—SAME AS CASH

ALL MEAT CUT BY APPOINTMENT

146 / Meat Eaters are Threatened

U.S. Government inspected—USDA Graded

Commercial beef guaranteed tender and delicious.

This is the typical hard sell of a freezer beef company. Anyone who has ever bought U.S. Commercial grade beef knows it's not tender and it's certainly not considered delicious (not even by the federal government). This is the type of fraudulent practice you must avoid. Chickens and other meat products have no government grade listed. Who knows where the company purchased its other advertised products? These establishments and others like them do everything they can to make a dollar, and unlike a national chain, they have no need to worry about the company image.

It's difficult to say which retail supermarkets are the best. Some may handle and process most food with special care, while others may mishandle most foods. Usually national food chains will do a little better than independent food chains in some areas. But from the hundreds of adulterations I have observed in 60 supermarkets with 8 different companies in the past decade, I question whether many good things could be said about retail supermarkets. They do usually buy a large percentage of government-inspected products.

Be especially leery of the rock-bottom bargain retail establishments with their wild, wild specials. When it comes to your health, don't cut corners on food quality. Be very careful of the damaged-in-transit advertising approach. These stores find ways to buy goods which are sometimes damaged in stock or from fire sales. These stores also buy seconds, nongovernment-inspected food products and low-grade products. If you love your family and want to protect their health, I do not recommend these establishments to you.

What Should Retail Meat Establishments Do?

All companies should establish the importance of health and sanitation to their employees and customers in their customer policy.

All companies should establish the importance of never adulterating food products for the sake of gross profit.

All companies should establish a universal terminology for the various cuts of meat so the consumer knows what he is buying.

All companies should refrain from gimmicks, hard sell or price leaders if they are not genuine.

All companies should use the clear see-through food containers for all processed meats.

All companies should label ground meat items by their relative fat content.

All companies should establish in writing a comprehensive program for health and sanitation similar to that used in USDA-inspected plants.

All companies should police their stores to make sure individual stores are complying with company policy on health and sanitation procedures.

All companies should establish a universal fresh dating code which allows the consumer knowledge of old or outdated foods. Correct rotation of all food products will save the companies money in the long run.

What Could Comprise a Comprehensive Health and Sanitation Program?

All persons who come in contact with food should be required to carry a health card requiring a complete physical examination, including a chest X-ray and blood test.

There should be strict temperature control for all perishable meat products. For the best protection from bacteria growth and related discoloration and spoilage, meat temperatures in the meat cooler should be kept near the freezing point between 28 to 35 degrees Fahrenheit. Meat should not be left out of refrigeration.

Cutting rooms should not exceed 48 degrees Fahrenheit to keep down bacteria growth as much as possible. The temperature control will save the companies thousands of dollars they are losing due to shrinkage and a short case-life leading to product putrefication from high bacteria counts. And it would discourage the adding of rotten meat to good meat for gross profit.

There should be employee training programs concerned with proper personal hygiene, sanitation practices and product wholesomeness. This would help cut down the increase of some food poisonings. It is inconceivable why the most technologically advanced country, with one of the highest standards of living in the world, allows so much public abuse. The companies could save money if their employees knew more about proper food care and sanitation practices.

Companies should use only approved germicidal solutions and refrain from using harsh detergents which could affect the public health when used on food processing equipment.

If all equipment used for food processing were cleaned with hot water, a germicidal cleaner, sanitized, and rinsed at least daily, the retail meat business would realize increased profit, because bacteria is the meat industry's biggest enemy, causing all meat items to spoil. The public would certainly be benefited, for they would receive a fresher product free from contamination and disease. Floors, walls, and meat display cases should be cleaned with a germicide solution and hot water and rinsed at least once a week.

If all equipment were cleaned and oiled each day, the companies would gain increased service life from machinery.

Sawdust shouldn't be used in meat department cutting rooms because it is often highly contaminated when first placed on the floor, and the longer it lays there, the more contaminated it becomes. The U. S. Department of Agriculture advises that sawdust should not be used in meat cutting rooms.

Meat products, including box items, should not be placed directly on the surface of the floor. If meat falls on the floor, it should be thrown away.

If retail meat establishments are looking for information on the latest methods for protection from spoilage, they could contact the Wholesaling and Retailing Branch, Transportation and Facilities Division and Field Crops and Animal Product Branch, Market Quality Research Division, Agricultural Research Service, United States Department of Agriculture.

Advice to the Consumer

Always do your grocery shopping last when you have a series of stops. Additional stops on the way home only compound the dangers of increasing bacteria growth because of high temperatures.

Purchase frozen foods and refrigerated meats last.

Always put meat away first when you arrive home from the market.

All pork or pork products should be cooked so that all the meat sections reach a temperature of not less than 150 degrees Fahrenheit. (The only exception would be pork that has been processed or treated to destroy trichinosis organisms.) If you don't have a thermometer, be certain that the pork has no trace of pink meat.

Watch that holiday turkey. Turkey is highly susceptible to salmonella poisoning, so be sure to cook it thoroughly to 165 degrees Fahrenheit to kill all the organisms. You should purchase a thermometer, because it's important that the turkey be thoroughly cooked. Stuffing should be prepared just before cooking the bird. All leftovers should be placed in the refrigerator immediately. Whenever you reheat any leftovers, make sure they are hot, not warm; this means heat to 140 degrees or above to kill bacteria.

If you notice a can with a swollen top, bottom, or sides, throw it away, or take it back to the store manager. Don't take a chance with your life. In many cases botulism causes cans to swell. Remember, botulism can grow in a vacuum.

Don't take a chance on spreading staph poisoning or some other food-borne illness because of improper care of an infection.

Never prepare food unless you wash your hands first. Wash them again after touching meat items, so you don't contaminate breads, desserts, or salads. Colds and sore throats may be transmitted by failure to wash hands before handling foods.

Remember that bacteria grows between 45 and 140 degrees Fahrenheit, so always keep food under refrigeration, especially food which has just been cooked.

Don't leave food out to cool after cooking or eating. This causes food to sour. Refrigerate promptly. Souring of foods is caused by contamination or spoilage organisms which survive the cooking process.

Don't forget that you do not know how long the supermarket stored meat items before you purchased them, so don't keep them too long. Most lunch meats should not be kept in your refrigerator longer than five days. Make sure you smell them before eating, and if they smell or feel slimy, don't eat them.

Be careful of ground meats like hamburger (ground beef), ground chuck, ground round, and ground sausage, because air has already started working on these meats. And the mill screw and cutting heads probably have contaminated the meat because this equipment is usually not cleaned more than once a week.

Canned hams should be checked when purchased. If they say "Keep under refrigeration," be sure the supermarket has followed those instructions. Many do not.

It would be best to patty and freeze ground meats as soon as you arrive home from the supermarket. The best advice, mentioned earlier, would be to grind your own ground meat items.

Uncooked, cured pork will last longer than fresh pork; but watch the fat, because it usually becomes putrefied first.

Bacon will last longer than most other meats. This is also true of other smoked and cured meats. Bacon should be eaten within a week of purchase.

Remember that temperatures in refrigeration deviate with the location of the storage compartments. The coolest area is under the freezing unit. Store meat salads in small shallow containers. Keep all meat dishes covered so that food particles from other shelves don't contaminate the meat.

Once frozen food has thawed, it starts to spoil very fast. It's best to use these foods as soon as possible, and, as a rule, never refreeze frozen foods.

Use a good-quality freezer paper and, if you plan to keep frozen food long, double-wrap it to protect it from freezer burn.

Let's Stop Polluting Our Bodies

In the past few years America has become cognizant of the hazards of air, water, noise, and solid pollution to the public health.

At the same time, although it is not widely known, we have been internally polluting our bodies with adulterated meats. Medical experts and the U.S. Food and Drug Administration estimate that there are about 2 million unreported cases of salmonella food poisoning alone in the United States every year.

The great majority of cases of all types of food poisoning—including salmonella, staph, shigella, and clostridium perfringens—go unreported, with the victim thinking it was the 24-hour flu, some virus, or just something they ate. In most cases it was something they ate—contaminated food. These types of food poisoning could be fatal in babies, old people, and those who are already sick. There are other food-borne illnesses polluting our bodies. It is estimated that 40 percent of all human diseases are contracted through food.[1]

Some other diseases that can be contracted through food are typhoid fever, streptococcus (septic sore throat), undulant fever, and dysentery.

Because of the convenience foods bought in meat delicatessens, many housewives are buying hundreds of prepared salads, desserts, and meat items instead of preparing these foods themselves; thus they are leaving themselves open to the dangers of contamination.

The retail meat business is contributing more than its fair share to this health problem because of very poor health and sanitation procedures in its delicatessens and meat departments.

The retail meat business has also used fraudulent advertising and sales gimmicks in the past to bring in customers. The states must resolve the manpower and appropriation shortages in retail inspection and give the public at least inspection equal to what is now found in the wholesale meat business. The large and small retail meat establishments must think about the public health. They have so far been concerned mainly with gross profit and the almighty dollar, and it is time they were more concerned about the public.

FOLLOW-UP READINGS

Bernarde, Melvin A. *The Chemicals We Eat.* New York, American Heritage Press, 1971.

Benenson, Abram S. *Control of Communicable Disease in Man.* 11th ed., 1970.

Hunter, Beatrice Trum. *Consumer Beware!* New York, Simon and Schuster, 1971.

Longgood, William. *The Poisons in Your Food.* New York, Simon and Schuster, 1960: Pyramid Books, 1970.

Gene Marine/Judith Allen, *Food Pollution: The Violation of Our Inner Ecology,* (New York: Holt, Rinehart and Winston, 1972).

The Safety of Foods: An International Symposium on the Safety and Importance of Foods in the Western Hemisphere. Westport, Conn., Avi Publishing Company, 1963.

Turner, James S. *The Chemical Feast* with an introduction by Ralph Nader. New York, Grossman, 1970.

Winter, Ruth. *Poisons in Your Food* with an introduction by Senator Walter F. Mondale. New York, Crown Publishers, 1969.

Hearings

Hearings before the House Select Committee to Investigate the Use of Chemicals in Foods & Cosmetics. 81st Congress, 1st session, 1950; 82nd Congress, 1st session, Parts 1 & 2, 1951; and Hearings before a Subcommittee of the Committee on Interstate & Foreign Commerce, on Food Additives, 85th Congress, 1957-58, Parts 1, 2 & 3.

154 / Meat Eaters are Threatened

Hearings before the Committee on Interstate and Foreign Commerce, House of Representatives, on Color Additives. 86th Congress, 2nd session, 1960.

Hearings before the Subcommittee on Reorganization and International Organizations of the Committee on Government Operations, United States Senate, Interagency Coordination in Environmental Hazards (Pesticides). Parts 1-7, 1963, Part 8, 1964: and Appendix 1-6 to Part 1.

Hearings before the Subcommittee on Antitrust & Monopoly of the Committee on the Judiciary, United States Senate, on Packaging & Labeling Legislation. 88th Congress, 1st session, Parts 1-3, 1963-64.

Hearings before a Subcommittee of the Committee on Agriculture and Forestry, United States Senate, 90th Congress, 1st session on S. 2147, S. 2218, and H.R. 12144. Bills to clarify and otherwise amend the meat inspection act, to provide cooperation with appropriate state agencies with respect to state meat inspections programs, and for other purposes.

Hearings before the Consumer Subcommittee of the Committee on Commerce, United States Senate. 90th Congress, 2nd session on S. 2958. To regulate interstate commerce by amending the federal food, drug, and cosmetic act to provide for the inspection of facilities used in the harvesting and processing of fish and fishery products for commercial purposes, for the inspection of fish and fishery products, and for cooperation with the States in the regulation of intrastate commerce with respect to state fish inspection programs and for other purposes; S. 3064. To amend the fish and wildlife act of 1956, as amended, to provide technical and financial assistance to the commercial fishing industry in meeting the requirements of the wholesale fish and fishery products act of 1968.

Hearings before the Subcommittee on Agricultural Research and General Legislation of the Committee on Agriculture and Forestry, United States Senate. 91st Congress, 2nd session on S. 3512, S. 3592, and S. 3603, Bills to exempt custom slaughtering operations from the meat inspection act and authorize interstate shipment of meat and meat products inspected by approved state meat inspection services.

NOTES

CHAPTER II

1. This inspection is described in a letter signed by meat employees working in Wethersfield Connecticut, April 17, 1971.
2. *A Strategy For A Liveable Environment*: A report to the Secretary of Health, Education and Welfare, Task Force on Environmental Health and Related Problems, June, 1967.
3. From a letter signed by four employees working in a Wethersfield Meat Deli in Wethersfield, Connecticut, May 15, 1971: "Poor Health and Sanitation in Meat Preparation Areas."
4. Ruth Winter, *Poisons in Your Food*, (New York: Crown Publishers, Inc., 1969), p. 165.
5. From a letter, "Meat Inspection," signed by three employees working in a Wethersfield market, Wethersfield, Connecticut, June 12, 1971.
6. *Op. cit.*, p. 209.
7. *The New York Times*, January 27, 1968. p. 1, col. 1.
8. Public Act 626, an act adopting the Model State Meat and Poultry Products Inspection Act, effective October 1, 1969, p. 15.
9. Philip R. Lee, M. D., Assistant Secretary of Health and Scientific Affairs, Department of Health, Education and Welfare, testimony before the Consumer Subcommittee, Committee on Commerce, U. S. Senate, April 23-25, 1968, p. 23.
10. *Ibid.*
11. *Ibid.*, pp. 22-23.
12. Harold E. Crowther, Director of the Bureau of Commercial Fisheries, U. S. Department of Interior, testimony before the Consumer Subcommittee, Committee on Commerce, U. S. Senate, July 20-21, 1967, pp. 20-21.
13. "Frozen Dinners," *Consumer Reports*, October 1967, O. 521.
14. "Frozen Fish Sticks," *Consumer Reports*, September 1970, p. 545.
15. "Food Dating: Now You See It, Now You Don't," *Consumer Reports*, June 1972, p. 394.
16. Op. cit., p. 547.

156 / *Meat Eaters are Threatened*

17. James L. Goddard, Commissioner of Food and Drugs, testimony before the Consumer Subcommittee, Committee on Commerce, U. S. Senate, April 23-25, 1968, p. 35.
18. Gene Marine/Judith Van Allen, *Food Pollution: The Violation of Our Inner Ecology,* (New York: Holt, Rinehart and Winston, 1972), p. 272.
19. Statement of Philip R. Lee M.D., Assistant Secretary of Health and Scientific Affairs, Department of Health, Education and Welfare, before the Consumer Subcommittee of the Committee on Commerce, U. S. Senate, April 23-25, 1968, p. 22.
20. *Ibid.,* p. 22-23.
21. Ruth Winter, *Poisons in Your Food,* (New York: Crown Publishers, Inc., 1969), pp. 109-110.
22. James L. Goddard, M. D., *Nutrition Today,* "Incident at Selby Junior High School." September 1967, p. 3.

CHAPTER III
1. From a letter signed by eight meat cutters at a national chain store in New Britain, Connecticut, July 3, 1971.
2. "A Close Look at Hamburger," *Consumers Reports,* August 1971, p. 479.
3. *Ibid.*
4. From a letter signed by seven meat cutters at a national chain store in New Britain, Connecticut, July 3, 1971.
5. *The Public Health Code of the State of Connecticut and other Department Regulations,* State Health Department, April 1970, p. 57.
6. *Ibid.*
7. *Ibid.*
8. *Ibid.*
9. *Ibid.,* p. 58.
10. *Ibid.*
11. *Ibid.,* p. 59
12. Abram S. Benenson, Ed., *Control of Communicable Diseases in Man,* 11th ed. (New York: American Public Health Association, 1970), pp. 256-257.
13. *Trichinosis Surveillance Annual Summary,* U.S. Department of Health, Education and Welfare, Public Health Service, National Communicable Disease Center, Atlanta, Georgia, July 1968, p. 1.
14. *Op. cit.,* p. 8.

CHAPTER IV
1. Ruth Winter, *Poisons in Your Food,* (New York: Crown Publishers, Inc., 1969), p. 119.
2. *Ibid.*
3. *Ibid.,* p. 123.
4. *Ibid.,* p. 124.

Notes / 157

5. As quoted in Beatrice Trum Hunter, *Consumer Beware*, (New York: Simon and Schuster, 1971), p. 136.
6. *Salmonella Surveillance Annual Summary*, U.S. Department of Health, Education and Welfare, Public Health Service, Health Services and Mental Health Administration, Center for Disease Control, Atlanta, Georgia, Published June 8, 1971, p. 1.
7. "Tuna Fish, the Favorite Canned Seafood," *Consumer Reports*, February 1964, p. 82.
8. Ruth Winter, *Poisons in Your Food*, (New York: Crown Publishers, Inc., 1969), pp. 127-128. See also Ralph W. Johnson, John Feldman and Rosemary Sullivan, *Public Health Reports*, July 1963, names were fictitious.
9. Abram S. Benenson, Ed. *Control of Communicable Diseases in Man*, 11th ed, (New York: American Public Health Association, 1970), pp. 220-221.
10. *Ibid.*
11. "Milk and Food," Report of the Committee on Environment Health Problems to the Surgeon General, U.S. Department of Health, Education and Welfare, Public Health Service, Washington, D.C.: USGPO, 1962, p. 136.
12. *Ibid.*, p. 142.
13. *Federal Register*, 35, Department of Agriculture, Consumer and Marketing Service, October 3, 1970, p. 15597.
14. Missouri Senate Bill 77, 74th General Assembly, An Act Relating to Livestock and poultry inspections, with penalty provisions, p. 1.
15. "A Close Look at Hamburger," *Consumer Reports*, August 1971, p. 478.
16. Federal Register, 35, U.S. Department of Agriculture, Consumer and Marketing Service, October 3, 1970, p. 15553.

CHAPTER V
1. Federal Register, 35, U.S. Department of Agriculture, Consumer and Marketing Service, October 3, 1970, p. 15599.
2. "The Great Ham Robbery," *Consumer Reports*, March 1961, p. 120-125.
3. "Hearings on Watered Hams," *Consumer Reports*, July 1961, p. 427.
4. "U.S. Loses a Test on Watered Hams," *The New York Times*, February 9, 1962.

CHAPTER VI
1. Article used by Mr. Ralph Nader from *The National Provisioner*, April 20, 1963 in testimony before the U.S. Senate Subcommittee on Agriculture and Forestry, November 14, 1967, p. 153.
2. Betty Furness, Special Assistant To The President For Consumer Affairs, testimony before the U.S. Senate Subcom-

158 / Meat Eaters are Threatened

    mittee on Agriculture and Forestry, November 9-14, 1967. p. 226.
3. Ralph Nader, testimony before the U.S. Senate Subcommittee on Agriculture and Forestry, November 14, 1967, pp. 152-153.
4. *Ibid.*, Quote from Nader referring to Dr. Stanford Mesrill's statements three weeks before Nader's testimony. Dr. Mesrill works for the Maine Department of Agriculture. Found on p. 153 of Senate Hearings. Note: Dr. Mesrill did not make the comments during the Senate Hearings.
5. Excerpts are assembled from the *Packing House Worker*, referred to as a Union Newspaper by Arnold Mayer, Legislative Representative, Amalgamated Meat Cutters' and Butchers' Workmen of North America, AFL-CIO, before the U.S. Senate Subcommittee on Agricultural and Forestry, November 14, 1967, p. 178-181.
6. Ralph Nader letter, submitted in testimony before the Subcommittee on Livestock and Grains; Committee on Agriculture, House of Representatives, July 20, 1967, pp. 242-250.
7. *Ibid.*, 160.
8. *Ibid.*
9. Information obtained from Barbara Lloyd, Center For The Study of Responsive Law, Washington, D.C. March 5, 1973.

Chapter VII
1. Upton Sinclair, *The Jungle*, (New York: The Viking Press, 1947).
2. Personal unwarned inspection by the Author, National Packing Company, Main Street, Hartford, Connecticut, June 23, 1971.

Chapter VIII
1. "Truth in Advertising: Supermarket Specials," *Consumer Reports*, August 1971, p. 466.
2. "Meatcutter Bares Traps For Unwary Shopper," *The Daily Democrat*, Woodland-Davis, California, May 31, 1973.
3. *Ibid.*

Chapter IX
1. "Quote Without Comment," *Consumer Reports*, May 1963, p. 206.

Chapter X
1. Harvey W. Wiley, *Influence of Food Preservatives and Artificial Colors on Digestion and Health*, U.S. Department of Agriculture, Bulletin 84 (1904).

2. "Controls Likely Against Antibiotic Residue," *Health Bulletin*, August 27, 1966, p. 2.
3. "A Close Look at Hamburger," *Consumer Reports*, August 1971, p. 478.
4. *Statistical Abstract of the United States*, 91st ed., U.S. Department of Commerce, (Washington, D.C. Printing Office, 1970), p. 83.
5. William Longgood, *The Poisons in Your Food*, (New York: Pyramid Books, 1970), p. 110.
6. *Ibid.*, p.p. 110-111.
7. *Ibid.*, 109.
8. "A Close Look at Hamburger," *Consumer Reports*, August 1971, p. 479.

CHAPTER XI
1. Ruth Winter, *Poisons in Your Food*, (New York: Crown Publishers, Inc., 1969), p. 141.